MORE POWER TO YOU

Get Recharged and Empowered for Ministry

MORE POWER TO YOU

Get Recharged and Empowered for Ministry

T.F. TENNEY

Treasure House

An Imprint of

Destiny Image® Publishers, Inc.
P.O. Box 310
Shippensburg, PA 17257-0310

"For where your treasure is, there will your heart be also."
Matthew 6:21

ISBN 0-7684-5005-5

For Worldwide Distribution
Printed in the U.S.A.

This book and all other Destiny Image, Revival Press, MercyPlace,
Fresh Bread, Destiny Image Fiction, and Treasure House books are
available at Christian bookstores and distributors worldwide.

For a U.S. bookstore nearest you, call **1-800-722-6774**.
For more information on foreign distributors, call **717-532-3040**.
Or reach us on the Internet:
www.destinyimage.com

ENDORSEMENTS

My friend and brother T.F. Tenney has that special gift of revelation to get to the key issue—the bottom line—and not take all day to do it. I know the way this strongly anointed man of God preaches and writes. I saw in his first six words, "The power is in the clay," that he had already reached me. I knew, also, after reading the title of his book, that I was going to read every page. I smiled and spoke out loud to myself: "Oral, T.F. has you again. He's going to probe, search, reveal your innermost being to yourself. Yet his words will land as softly as a mother's love on your emotions." I guarantee you one thing: you will know as never before that God's power is already in you. There's just one thing—and only one—that's really important to your life, and this friend and brother in the Lord—a truly gifted writer—will take you by the hand and show you the way to bring it forth.

—Oral Roberts

CONTENTS

FOREWORD

I have long ago given up hope on getting the "last word in" with this author. So I'll take my liberty with making sure I get the *first* word in!

Whenever I think I've made some "new" discovery in the Word of God, and excitedly begin to share it with my dad, T.F. Tenney, I often realize that my "new" revelation is old news to him. Dad then goes on to elaborate and carry the torch of fresh oil much further in the Scriptures than I ever imagined.

Incredibly what T F. Tenney uncovers from God's Word is not some impractical bit of scriptural trivia. Interesting but useless! His understandings help in the day-to-day struggles of life.

Have you ever needed more power? Let me introduce you to my earthly father, who will make the proper introduction to our Heavenly Father, the secret source of *all* power!

Almost every time I speak, and in everything I write, there is a quote from my dad, T.F. Tenney. Most of the time it is an unconscious quote. I repeat something that I learned from him many years ago without even "sourcing" my quote. This is not an "on purpose" slighting of my father. It is the arrogance of my own knowledge. He did such a thorough job teaching me the concepts of the Word of God, I don't even remember *not* knowing some things that Dad taught me.

This book, *More Power to You*, will "charge" your life! T.F. Tenney's writings are "shocking" truths! This book is meant to empower you by hooking you up the true source of all power, the Word of God. When the two-edged Word of God is handled by a skilled swordsman, the end result is life-changing revelation. T.F. Tenney is just such a swordsman.

Handle this book carefully, read it closely; it's so sharp it *could* cut you!

—Tommy Tenney
Author, GodChaser

INTRODUCTION

As noted in *Secret Sources of Power*, the dictionary definition of that five-letter word is somewhat simple: "The ability or capacity to perform or act effectively." However, complexity enters the picture when one realizes that the source of real power is limitless and our need for Him is without measure.

This book, like the one before it, is the product of various sermons preached throughout fifty years of Apostolic ministry. As much as possible I have tried to make note of sources and resources. However, if I have overlooked someone or something, please know that it is unintentional and simply an indication that their work has become such a part of the fabric of my ministry there is difficulty separating the threads.

You hold in your hands keys to achieving "the ability or capacity to perform or act effectively." You'll see—as you read through it—that power often displays itself in unusual places and unique ways. There is power in clay—and as I heard one old preacher proclaim, we're all just glorified mudballs! There is power in a crumb—and spectacular power in Him who is the bread of life! This book invites you to explore the Source of all power—while discovering there is power in His glory—and power in His name—and power in His Spirit! More power to you!

CHAPTER 1

THE POWER OF THE CLAY

The word which came to Jeremiah from the Lord,
saying, Arise, and go down to the potter's house,
and there I will cause thee to hear My words. Then
I went down to the potter's house, and, behold, he
wrought a work on the wheels (Jeremiah 18:1-3).

The power is in the clay! When observing a potter working with his wheel, one might take for granted that the power is in the wheel—a monotonous going-in-circles energy. Or, one might consider the source of the power to be in the movement of the foot and treadle—a spinning force. Then again, possibly the strength is in the hands of the potter, as he shapes and molds the clay. But to the careful observer, the absolute power—the real power—rests in the clay. For it is in the clay that we find the power of yielding, the power of becoming. The best potter, the most skilled craftsman, cannot do anything with clay that refuses to be molded. The power to become—and the power to resist—is in the clay.

You Must Learn Your Lesson

When the Lord spoke to Jeremiah as recorded in the passage above, an interesting phrase was used. He said, "...I will cause thee to hear My words." Sometimes we are listening, intentionally and intently. At other times, God must "cause" us to listen. Perhaps we are not in the right frame of mind to hear Him, or maybe just not prepared to understand Him. Often in our lives, He must give us illustrated lessons, such as He did here with Jeremiah. When God wants to teach you faithfulness, He will lead you through an experience to give you the opportunity to learn its definition. There is a vast difference between knowing something and learning it. You can know something in your head, but it is only when you "learn your lesson" that it becomes a part of your heart. When you bring knowing to learning, you bring the lesson into the living level of your personal experience. God doesn't want us just to know; He wants us to learn.

> WHEN YOU BRING knowing to learning, you bring the lesson into the living level of your personal experience.

God guides us through life experiences that turn words into lessons learned. The word of the Lord to Jeremiah was to go to the potter's house. When Jeremiah arrived there, he saw something. What he saw became a word from the Lord to him. Whether you will hear the word of the Lord or not often depends on what you are looking for.

Back to the Basics

Then I went down to the potter's house, and, behold, he wrought a work on the wheels. And the vessel that he made of clay was marred in the hand of the potter: so he made it again another vessel, as seemed good to the potter to make it. Then the word of the Lord came to me, saying, O house of Israel, cannot I do with you as this potter? saith the Lord. Behold, as the clay is in the potter's hand, so are ye in mine hand, O house of Israel (Jeremiah 18:3-6).

At first glance, this scene probably seemed quite ordinary to the old prophet. I have personally visited in the Mid-East and have watched potters working the clay in the old-time way. I've seen them carefully form a vase then perceive some flaw with their fingertips that I as a casual observer could not detect. The next thing I knew the clay was crushed on the wheel, and the potter began again his painstaking work.

As the prophet was lamenting about Israel and their situation, he heard "Arise, Jeremiah, and go face reality." God said, "Let me show you the root of the problem" and took him to watch again something he had no doubt been seeing since he was just a boy. It was something so basic and primary. A potter. A wheel. Clay.

It is dangerous to get away from the basics of God, to forget in the froth and foam of life what is real. The vital issues of life are not on the peripheral edges; sometimes it is necessary for God to take us back to the basics.

Can you imagine what Jeremiah must have thought when he first heard the command to go to the potter's house? It was as tasteless as sand. "What can I learn there I don't already know? I've watched that old potter more times than I can count. Why, Lord, I can even tell You exactly how they operate. But You said to go, so go I will." Jeremiah was about to learn that God some-times works in circles.

Walking in Circles

Have you ever gotten caught in one of God's eddies? Israel marched around the same mountain for 40 years until they learned what God wanted them to learn. It was a difference between knowing and learning. Once it was *learned* God released them. Once the old Egyptian flesh died and was buried, He set them free from their trek around the mountain. Have you ever felt like you were marching round and round your own mountain? I could give guided tours!

It's monotonous. And it is very, very dangerous. It is easy to get disillusioned with the routine, the tedious sameness of it, and instead try to make something happen. Spiritual vertigo can be destructive. The fact is, most of our walking with God is rou-tine. It is not spectacular. It is not fireworks and awe-inspiring displays. It is the slow steady burn of a single flame. The power of routine is what saved Daniel. He prayed every day. He didn't pray more in crisis; he didn't pray less in ease. His prayer nei-ther sped up nor slowed down the process.

In a strikingly familiar passage, another prophet wrote, "They that wait upon the Lord..." (Is. 40:31) ...shall do what? Notice the *progression* in that passage is reverse of what we ordinarily think. He said, "mount up with wings as eagles"; then "run, and not be weary"; then "walk, and not faint." We auto-matically want to start walking, then accelerate to a run, then take wing and fly. God says, "No, that's not My way. You may start off flying, then you'll come down to running, but most of the time you'll be walking." It's consecrated plodding. One foot in front of the other. That's not to say there will not be those high-flying, ecstatic experiences. They simply are the exception, not the rule. Where you finally end up is in the very basic skill of walking with God.

A Set Foundation for Each Generation

We cannot afford to tamper with the basic, foundational issues. Paul said, "Leaving the foundation, go on to maturity and perfection" (see Heb. 6:1). He didn't mean to tear the foundation up and start all over again without it. He was saying that we must acknowledge some things are settled. They are foundational. Once the foundation is set, you begin to build. The superstructure may vary. How many rooms—where you put the walls—those things are open for discussion. However, the foundation is set. "If the foundations be destroyed, what can the righteous do?" (Ps. 11:3) These truths, though they may appear to be tiresomely monotonous, though their changelessness can perhaps frustrate, are foundational—basic to a successful life with God. We are built on the foundation of the apostles and prophets.

Each generation must experience God for themselves. God has no grandchildren. While our children may inherit our organizations, our finances, or our buildings, they cannot inherit our experience with God. The foundational structure of the Kingdom remains firm and must be learned by each succeeding generation, as they embark upon building a structure for their own generation.

The Power of the Clay

God started out as a potter in the Garden of Eden. He formed man out of clay. He knows more about the pottery business and the pottery process than anyone. He commanded Jeremiah to go to the potter's house for the purpose of learning a lesson. So Jeremiah went. As he watched the potter put the clay on the wheel. He saw him mold it and shape it into some type of vessel. Then he watched as the vessel became marred, causing the potter to start the process over again. The wheel was willing. The potter was willing. But the power to become was in whether or not the clay would yield to what the master potter had in mind. When the vessel became marred, it was not the fault of the wheel. The wheel was doing what it was supposed to be doing. Neither can we blame the potter. The potter was experienced and highly skilled. He knew what he was doing. The power was in the clay.

The God of a Second Chance

The Bible continues the story and recounts how the potter "made it again." I believe God has a perfect pattern for our lives—a design for what He wants us to become. He places us on the wheel and begins the process of molding and shaping us into His image. When we can't cooperate—or rather, don't cooperate—and the power to become is limited by what we will allow, He is patient. He does not throw us away. He says, "I will make it again."

In the olden times of skilled craftsmen, the potter always had a second vessel in mind. It might not have been as beautiful or as useful as the first, but potters were committed to trying again. The vessel might never have been what it could have been. Yet, willing to get back on the wheel another time, even for *second best*, the clay still held within itself the power to become.

I want to be what God has always wanted me to be. Yet my prayer is, "Lord, if I don't yield or if I forget the basics, then please don't throw me in the potter's field. Put me on the wheel again. Find a place for me—somewhere." It is a prayer He will answer.

Most potters give clay three chances. If after three attempts to mold clay the potter is still unsuccessful, he abandons the process. The clay is left unmolded and unusable. God, on the other hand, never gives up on us. He is always willing to put us back on the wheel and make us again. He is the God of a second chance.

God's Will for the Clay

Remember this somewhat simplistic thought: Evolutionists take us back to animals; God goes further back than the evolutionists and takes us to mud. We might think we are "really something"—but we are nothing but a glorified mud ball.

The difference between mud and the vase is the clay. From mud ball to vessel of usefulness, the power is in the clay whether to yield to the design that is in the Master's mind. "We have this treasure in earthen vessels…" (2 Cor. 4:7). This treasure is in a house of clay. God has deposited Himself in each of us with the infilling of His Spirit. In Jeremiah 29:11, the Lord said, "I know the thoughts that I think toward you…to give you an expected end." One translation says, "…a bright future and hope…"

God did not just fling you out in the nebulous of life and forget you. He has a plan for you. He has a will for your life. He doesn't play divine games of hide-and-seek. We are not pawns on some cosmic sacred chessboard. Too often we think the will of God is an elusive idea. I personally believe that He wants to make His will known to us sometimes even more desperately than we claim to be seeking to know His will.

Our problem is not finding the will of God, it is in doing the will of God. A lot of what we call trying to find God's will is actually trying to change God's mind. He has a plan but too often we have a mind-set—a preconceived notion of what we want to do and who we want to be. So, we pray and pray and maybe even fast a day or two. We try to change God's mind, to convince Him our plan is better than His.

Prophetically, the passage in Jeremiah was a message to Israel. They would not yield. They resisted much like the clay on the observed potter's wheel. It hardened and would not yield to the ministrations of the potter. It fell apart in his hands. God was trying to convey to Jeremiah—and then to Israel— that the power to be was within them. God is not an unwilling God. You don't pray to get God in a good mood. You don't pray to purchase power with Him to buy your own way. Days of fasting don't add purchase power to your prayers. You pray—and you fast—to enhance your relationship with Him. When He places you on the wheel, He molds you into the best you can possibly be or become for Him.

Remember Pharaoh? He was a God-rejector. When human will clashes blatantly with God's will the result is often quite spectacular. God is determined to transform us but He will not violate or burglarize the human will. He will not force Himself on us. We must yield to Him.

When Pharaoh refused, the frogs came. He cried, "Oh, Moses, get this off us." The frogs disappeared. Yet Exodus 8:15 tells us, "But when Pharaoh saw that there was respite [or relief], he hardened his heart, and hearkened not...." Five times he hardened his heart and would not let the people go.

In Exodus, chapter 10, the Lord told Moses to go to Pharaoh, noting in advance, "...for I have hardened his heart." *God* hardened his heart? Rest assured God never hardens a man's heart before the man has hardened it himself.

A word of explanation here. The same sun that melts butter, also hardens clay. It is in the substance. It is not the sun. You must be melted before you can be molded. Sometimes God sends us into a meltdown. Everything seems to be falling apart. Financial dilemmas, family stresses, work issues make us physically and emotionally exhausted. We take the pieces and say, "Lord, please put me back together..." and unspoken but not unfelt is the specification, "...but put me back together again just like I was."

God will always give you the best if you leave the choice to Him. What we must do is bring our human mind and its frailties into submission to the mind of God. The divine mind and the human mind bring the flesh—the clay—under control. "Not my will, but Thine be done" is the prayer of a surrendered mind, heart, and will. It is the cry of moldable clay. It is the power cry of human surrender to divine intervention.

Your Final Surrender, Not the Struggle, Is What Matters to God

Everyone around Pharaoh told him to give up and give in. The servants told him. The magicians told him. It's even recorded that one time he himself cried out, "I've sinned." Yet he constantly rejected the pleas of Moses. Finally, he was totally hardened against the children of Israel and their cries. God sees the final choice, not just what intervenes between the initial encounter and the final decision. What counts with God is the final choice. Pharaoh could have turned around at the last plague and said, "I give in, God. Have Your way with us all." God would have forgotten all the times he hadn't yielded and honored the final determination.

So it continues to be with God and His children. We have all experienced times when self-will has wrestled against God's will. Yet when the yielding is finally done, the struggle is forgotten. The final relinquishment of self is what matters ultimately to God. "Not my will, but Thine be done" is not diluted by "If it be Thy will...let it pass...." The fact that when it comes down to the final drawing of lines I say, "Here I am Lord, what do You want me to do?" is all that is important to Him, not the process that brings us to that point of surrender.

I'd rather meet a fence at the top of a cliff than the ambulance at the bottom. Some things God positions in our way are protective measures. He wants us to turn out right. We'll never move mountains as long as we're satisfied to scrape the top off of anthills.

The prodigal son said, "Give me the goods." The Father simply said, "All right." Anytime you want back what you've given to God, He'll give it back to you. He wants no unwilling servants. If you don't want to be what God wants you to be, the power is yours to determine it. He is a God of fairness. He will not force you; He will not violate your desires or your will. God is fair.

God is fair? *Fair?* What about… ? Yes, He is fair. Let me show you.

"Blessed are the merciful: for they shall obtain mercy" (Mt. 5:7). If you want mercy, show mercy. How do you want to be judged by God? You will be judged by God according to how you judge everyone else. The same judgment you mete out is going to be meted out to you. Isn't that fair? God allows us to set our own judgment. Do you need forgiveness? Forgive.

Now the converse is also true…if you don't want to be forgiven, unforgiveness is fine. If you want or need no mercy, then there is no need to be merciful. And you will never know what you could have become if you had yielded to Him and His molding.

Do you recall the story of Achan? Can you imagine Joshua's consternation that day? They went out to battle, not even taking a full charge of warriors because he was so confident of impending victory. The people of Ai were few and victory seeming assured. Yet when all was said and done, the Israelites ran away defeated. Joshua rent his clothes and fell on his face before the Lord saying, "…Lord, why did You ever bring this people across the Jordan to deliver us into the hands of the Amorites to destroy us? If only we had been content to stay on the other side of the Jordan!" (see Josh. 7:7) But when the rest of the story was made known to Joshua and the elders, they realized the tragedy of one hardened heart was at the root of it all.

Achan had walked 40 years in the wilderness. He had cir-
cled the mountain. He had eaten the manna. He had seen the
pillar of cloud and followed the pillar of fire. But somewhere
along the way...just before time to cash in on a victory, he
caved in. He hardened his heart. In the final moments he lost
out because of self-will. What a tragic end to a man's life story.

Only when you give God your will, really surrender yourself to Him, can He become active in your life. When you kneel
at the altar under duress, it will not hold. Someone said we
need dedication and we need re-dedication. What we really
need is total surrender. When you surrender to Him, you surrender to the power of becoming what God wants you to
become.

Judas was only 51 days from having his name in the foundation of that City not made with hands. If he could have held
on for just 1,224 more hours, what a different end there would
be to his story. Instead, he ended up in a potter's field—despite
Jesus' giving him one last chance. Jesus said, "Whoever dips
with Me..." (see Mt. 26:23). What if he hadn't done it? What if,
at that point, he had yielded? His whole life's ending would
have been different and God would have counted only the surrender, not the struggle. Instead, the enemy entered his heart
and the power in the unsurrendered clay became death and
destruction.

Yielding to the Potter Brings Joy

I have often said, "Life is not doing what you want to do;
life is doing what you ought to do." Happiness is not doing
what you like as much as it is liking what you do. Yielding to

the Potter and allowing Him to make us what He designed us to be is the ultimate of eternal joy, rather than temporal happiness.

The Lord was trying to convey to Jeremiah that the problem didn't lie with God, but with the Israelites. He said, "Jeremiah, the problem is not Me. It's not you. It is these unyielding people." It was a basic message.

Sometimes life is tough. Rose petals falling on a rock never produce precious stones. Constant happiness never produces strong Christians. The Lord loves you too much to shield you from everything that is uncomfortable. I've heard some claim, "The Lord loves me like I am." Yes, He does. He also loves you too much to leave you that way. He will send things into our lives. Wheels. Sharp instruments to etch His impression on us. Have you ever wondered what it would be like if clay could talk? "Hey! Do you have to slap me around so much?" "What's with your fingers stretching me out like that?" "Watch it! I liked that bump!" Change hurts. Being made from our image into His doesn't happen without pain.

Jesus came to make disciples, not just to secure converts or church attendees. The word *disciple* comes from *discipline*. Both words are from the Latin *discipulus*, which means "pupil." According to the American Heritage Dictionary, the two primary definitions of *discipline* are: 1) "Training expected to produce a specific character or pattern of behavior, especially training that produces moral or mental improvement" and 2) "Controlled behavior resulting from disciplinary training; self-control." Disciples are, according to that authority, "active adherents" to a philosophy. To become a disciple is to embrace changes in our lives and hearts that will conform us to

His image. It affects our character, our behavior; it improves our morals, it improves our mental status, and it is an exercise in self-control. For we are no longer tossed about by the winds, but stand firm on the rock that is Christ Jesus.

He wants us to move from feelings to faith. From impulse to dedication. From infancy to maturity. From experience to a learned walk with God. From being an audience to being an army. To do that, we must learn to yield to God. The power is in the clay—the power is in us to yield, or not.

Under Pressure on the Wheel

I heard a story one time of a little boy who stood on the street corner and shined the shoes of willing passersby. He did a good job and many customers returned for his services. One morning, though, while busy at his work, his countenance was glum. The man whose shoes were being shined looked down and realized teardrops were falling from the boy's face onto his somewhat polished shoe. He jerked his foot back, and harshly said, "Boy, what's wrong with you? You're getting your salty tears on my shoe. I ought not give you another dime!" The boy looked up, tears still flowing, and said, "Sir, my mom died last night. I'm just trying to make enough money this morning to buy some flowers for her funeral." Tears sprung to the man's eyes. He gently removed the buffer from the boy's hand, wiped the last of the tears away, and pressed a ten-dollar bill into the boy's palm before going on his way. On the surface, the boy's service looked like a botched job. But, when the man knew the heart of the boy, it changed everything.

Too often we are too quick to judge. A brother or sister can be under pressure on the wheel, and we don't understand. God brings circumstances into our lives, not to break us, but to make us. Life is a grindstone. Whether it grinds you or polishes you depends on what you are made of and how you take it. The saying is, "Look on the bright side..." but sometimes the response is, "There isn't a bright side to this." In those times, our only hope is to polish up the dull side!

In my estimation the Lord probably hears the sound of the fifteenth letter of the alphabet more than any other human verbiage. "Oh! Ohhhhh! Oh, God!" The wheel is not always a comfortable place to be, but it is the only place to be as we become more like Him and more like what He wants us to be.

Mold us. Make us. Convict us. Convert us. Convince us. Commit us. Help us to be what we know we ought to be—and to allow You to send whatever circumstances are required for Your perfect will to be accomplished in us.

We need the power to become. He is saying to us, "The power to become is in you." The power is in the clay. We pray, "Lord, use me." We used to sing a chorus that said, "Jesus, use me. Please Lord, don't refuse me. Surely there's a work that I can do..." I promise if you will get in a position where God can use you, He will wear you out! However, it doesn't happen just by mouthing the words. You must place yourself in a position and condition where God can use you. When hardness of heart sets in, we can no longer distinguish between right and wrong, true and false. We cannot understand or even feel the hands of the Potter.

Have Faith in God's Wheel

There is an old adage that says, "For every problem under the sun, there is a solution or there is none. If there is one, seek until you find it. If there isn't one, never mind it." You can wear yourself out trying to get off the wheel He has sent to design you. A mark of maturity in Christ is to understand there are some problems that cannot be solved. You must just live through them. I've seen families who have messed up, then messed up again, then messed up again. Some have carried a load for years and short-circuited their ability to walk with God. You can't unring a bell, but you can stop it from tolling again and again.

What can you do about it? Leave it in the hands of God. Press on. Keep becoming what God wants you to be. There are many things in life we cannot change. You cannot go back and undo past mistakes. You can learn from them and not repeat them. The tragedy that often determines whether you are able to get past something or whether you will repeat the same mistake is doubt. If you doubt yourself, if you doubt God, if you doubt His ability to get you past your past—doubt wins, you lose.

Doubt is sick faith. From time to time in our lives we all experience doubt. There is a significant difference between doubt and unbelief. Unbelief says, "I'm not going to believe." But to doubt, you must first have had a measure of faith. Doubt only occupies space left by faith abandoned.

Occasionally our faith catches a "virus." First, a little doubt comes in and you have to deal with it. You have to return to the basics and have a personal confrontation with God. Seeing Him high and lifted up and knowing He is in control of everything in our lives can renew our faith—in Him and in ourselves. Ourselves? Yes, when it dawns on me that I am not in control, when I acknowledge that He is in control, my faith in His ability to use me and the circumstances of my life for His glory is renewed.

The Bible says, "Casting all your care upon Him; for He careth for you" (1 Pet 5:7). David wrote, "...I [have never] seen the righteous forsaken, nor his seed begging bread" (Ps. 37:25). The word *cast* in both the Hebrew and Greek means "to throw and let go. To throw in a particular direction, to be more specific, and let go." He said, "Throw it in God's direction and let loose of it."

In my part of the country (central Louisiana), the word cast brings to mind the whir-r-r-r and pop of a lure on the end of a casting rod as it hits the water. With a little wrist and elbow action we reel it right back in. We cast it—and reel it back in—and hopefully in the process attract a fish to the little lure and bring it back, too. So it is that in some of our altar experiences, we cast something on the Lord...then slowly but surely start reeling it back in to ourselves, having never truly surrendered it. Sure, we let it go long enough to make it look like it is being cast at His feet...but a strong chord of personal possession remains attached to it and we ultimately don't give anything to Him at all.

Stay on the Wheel Until You Conquer

We must reach an understanding in our hearts and minds as to what truly occurs to a person who is on His wheel. Sometimes something bad happens to us in life. We finally get over it and it happens again. And again. And again. And finally we say, "God, what's wrong? Why does this keep happening to me?" His answer is simple: "As soon as you learn what it is I am trying to teach you, we will go on to the next lesson. Until then, you will have to keep working on this one." Little irritating things (and big ones) will keep popping up. Stay on the wheel. He knows what He's doing, even when it is obscured from you and me.

Have you ever studied pearls? A pearl is a tribute to a conquered irritant. There is a little oyster on the bottom of the ocean doing exactly what it is supposed to be doing. It is cleansing the ocean—removing the algae while opening and closing. It is functioning in the exact plan and purpose of God for itself. All of a sudden, a grain of sand gets lodged. The oyster could say, "Oh, I have been so mistreated. I was just doing what I am supposed to be doing and now this! I am just going to clam up. I'm never opening again." But that's not the way it happens. The oyster takes that irritant and makes something beautiful and valuable of it and just keeps going. There will always be some kind of irritant that will get into our lives. We can either be bitter or better because of it. A pearl is a tribute to a conquered irritant.

Here's a humorous thought: People talk about the pearly gates as if they are gates covered with pearls when in fact, according to the Scripture, each gate is one pearl. Twelve gates each constructed of a single pearl. First, I'd like to see the oyster. Second, did that oyster ever have a problem!

Another lesson that comes to mind in this discussion of pearly gates is that you and I will pass through the gates of that

City through conquered problems. As you pass into that City not made with hands, you can with a shout declare, "I have conquered my last problem. I am passing through the gates and I have made it home!"

Softening the Clay

Don't harden your heart. Life has a way of grinding you up. Life has a way of stepping on you. I have been stomped on. I have been disappointed. People have lied about me. People have called me names. I have been given instruction I did not think I needed. I have been kicked in the appropriate portion of the anatomy. (Anytime people are kicking you in the rear, at least you know who's out front.) Trials come with life.

"The problem, Jeremiah, in this object lesson, is the clay. The problem is in Israel." God is not the problem. The circumstances are not the problem. The power to become is in the clay. Hardening of the heart is bad business.

David also sinned. Yet the minute Nathan said, "Thou art the man," David's heart was melted (see 2 Sam. 12:7-13). He could have said, "I am the king. I can do whatever I please. Nathan, be gone with you!" He could have given the order to hang the prophet who spoke words unpleasant to the king. But instead, he repented before God. You can prove you are a surrendered Christian when God puts a situation in your way which could mean almost life and death, and you choose to show mercy, not judgment.

David did not harden his heart. Consequently, when he said, "Lord, have mercy upon me according to Thy lovingkindness...according to the multitude of Thy tender mercies," He prayed according to God's mercy (see Ps. 51). He did not make excuses. All of us tend to think at times that the universe runs its axis right through our lives. Sometimes we envision our way of thinking as the present reality of God. But David simply threw himself on the mercies of God. He had been a man who had shown mercy. He then sought God to show mercy to him. "I acknowledge my transgression. My sin is ever before me." He did not hesitate to admit his guilt, nor to name his sin. He had sinned against Uriah and Bathsheba and the armies, but he took his guilt further still: "Against Thee and Thee only have I sinned."

Deep Down on the Inside

David said, "Thou desirest truth in the inward parts." He was transparently honest. It is not a question of "God, what do You want to know?" It is not only *what* I am doing but *why* I am doing it. "Truth in the inward parts" is a question about what we are deep down on the inside. When pressure is applied to our lives, what's on the inside of us is revealed.

In Acts when Stephen was being accused of blasphemy by the council, the Bible says his face shone like an angel (see Acts 6:15). Why? Because when they put pressure on him, as they were literally piling stones on him, what was inside him came out. When pressure is applied, whatever is on the inside will become evident. If you are full of the love of God, mercy, a love for the Word, a love for His Kingdom—that's what will appear. But if you are full of bad temper, unforgiveness, bitterness, fear—those things will display themselves under pressure as well.

Sometimes God applies pressure for self-revelation. We need to discover what is inside so we can correct it. Remember,

He wants truth in the inward parts. The only way we are able to judge people is outwardly—by what we see. I would easily agree that if a man is addicted to alcohol, as a pastor I would not want this individual as a choir member. However, I might have men and women in my choir who are full of pride. The liquor might smell worse to me, but the pride might smell worse to God.

God wants to know what we are made of deep down on the inside. He will put the Church in a position where He can find out. There is no need to find fault with the circumstances of your life. You can waste time blaming people, your background, your environment, your life situation. However, there are times in life when you just have to "finish the chapter." Regardless of how bad it is, or how bad it was—make an end to the chapter and be done with it—and get on with the rest of the book. The end of the chapter is not the end of the book.

Paul said, "Forgetting those things which are behind...I press toward the mark..." (Phil. 3:13b-14). Sometimes life requires that you forget the past and press to the future. If you drag all the garbage you have picked up in life behind you, you will not make much progress. Cut it loose and let it go. Jesus is a good garbage collector. He alone can make all things new.

Take the Blame

If you really want reconciliation in your life with a brother or sister who has wronged you, you must be willing to take 100 percent of the blame. "But it wasn't my fault. I didn't do it; why should I take the blame for it?" The question then is: Do you want to be a Christian? Jesus was not to blame but the Bible said He "hath laid on Him the iniquity of us all" (Is. 53:6b). He blamed Himself for my sin; He took my sin upon Himself. Jesus took the blame, yet He was not at fault. But, His action brought reconciliation between God and all of mankind. This is not necessarily what I am, but it is what I ought to be. Would I be willing to take unmerited blame to effect reconciliation?

Yet we continue to insist on *my* rights, *my* way, *my* say, *my* opinion, *my* choice. There are times when God will place you in a situation and you may have to take the blame.

Time and again I have witnessed situations where it appears someone is getting away with something. But the truth of the matter is, I have also lived long enough to see that sooner or later no one gets away with anything. It is simply a matter of timing. When David's men encountered the sleeping Saul, they said, "Let me at him! I'll take care of him for good!" David said, "Not only will I not do it myself, I will not let you do it" (see 1 Sam. 26:7-11). He knew God would take care of Saul in His time.

Henry VIII, caught in his sin, killed his wives. Caesar, too, killed his wives. Before them, David was a king with the power to take life. However, ultimately he said, "Have mercy on me! I did it. I have sinned!" He was a man after God's own heart. That's the power of the clay! Power to become what God intends for us to be, instead of what we would become on our own.

Standards That Set Ourselves Apart

To each of us is given the choice—the potter's wheel or the potter's field. If we are going to be a generation of men and women used by God, we must yield to His will and His way. God doesn't use us all the same way. Yet the foundational issues for each of us remain intact. Don't touch them. We may not all have the same type of ministry. We don't even all believe alike. (Attend a prophecy conference and you will see that there is much on which we disagree.) The question is are we willing to, on the wheel, be molded and remolded—yielding to His will and His way, which calls for unity in the midst of diversity?

Some people get pushed out of shape (after all, we are talking about clay here) over church discipline or standards. Standards are designed to be your guardrails. They aren't the highway; they are the barriers that mark its sides. I don't want to get on a highway that doesn't have guardrails. Nor do I want to use the railings as the road—you certainly cannot drive on them.

Study the epistles and see what professing, born-again Christian people are capable of doing. Why did Paul write to the church at Ephesus and say, "Let him that stole steal no more" (Eph. 4:28a) if there were no thieves among them? What were they doing at the Lord's table in Corinth, if they weren't imbibing a little too much, too long? Gluttony and neglect of others were present among them.

George Barna said in *The Second Coming of the Church*, "The Bible clearly states that true believers should be readily distinguished from nonbelievers by the way they live. Yet the evidence undeniably suggests that most American Christians today do not live in a way that is quantifiably different from those non-Christian peers in spite of the fact they profess to believe in a set of principles that should clearly set them apart" (pp. 120-121).

Sitting on the Shelf

The power to be is in the clay. Yet, when the potter takes the clay vessel off the wheel, the next place it goes is the fire. It is part of the process. Although we like the finished product, we may not like the process. From the fire it goes to the shelf to "cure." You haven't lived until God has put you on the shelf awhile. You cannot be made directly available for commerce. You cannot be used until you have been on the shelf a while. Sometimes, through trials, God just parks us. "In your patience, possess ye your souls" (Lk. 21:19).

> ALTHOUGH WE LIKE the finished product, we may not like the process.

I've been parked a few times in my life. I've wandered, "God, are you ever going to do something here?" It has been attributed to Smith Wigglesworth, who at a similar time in his life said, "Either God moves me or I move God, but something's got to give."

Why does He park us? To see what we are going to do. Are you going to blame everyone else? Blame the system? Blame the pastor? "I think I could teach this class, but Pastor just ignores me." Just sit there and cure awhile. When you're ready, God will see. Your gift will make room for itself.

The wheel, the hands of the potter, the heat, the shelf. It is all part of the process of what God has in mind for what He wants you to be. This treasure of God in an earthen vessel. Why shouldn't He try the vessels in which He intends to deposit eternal treasure?

I want to be a Christian before anything else. I want to be remembered by my family and closest associates, above everything else, as a Christian. To me, that is the highest title that can be given a man. It is up to me. The power is in the clay. Yield to Him and become.

Never Hearing "It Can't Be Done"

George Danzig was one of the world's leading mathematicians and served as head of the Department of Mathematics at Stanford University for many years. When he was a student, he had to study hard to make good grades. One night, for the final exam in Mathematics, which was his specialty, he pulled the well-known all-nighter studying. About dawn, his eyes heavy with sleep, he laid his head down on his desk and dozed off to later awaken with a start. Realizing he was late for class and his final examination, he jumped up, splashed water on his face, and literally ran to the classroom.

The class had already begun. As the professor handed him the test, he sat down and looked up on the board, where the professor had written three additional problems. When the time was up for the exam, he went to the professor and said, "Sir, I was late and I apologize. Would you give me a little extra time to work these three problems on the board? I've got them on a separate piece of paper." The professor smiled at him and said, "Yes, in fact, you've been a good student this semester. I'll give you until tomorrow." George Danzig worked all day and into the night on the problems and finally had to admit defeat. He went in and laid the paper on the teacher's desk with a note, "I could not work the third problem." He went back to his dorm room and fell into an exhausted sleep.

Later he was awakened by someone banging on his dormitory room door. "George! George! Wake up!" He stumbled to the door and there was his professor just about jumping up and down with excitement. "What is it, Professor?" "George, this is your paper?" "Yes, sir. I never could get the answer to that third problem. I'm sorry." "George, my boy! You don't understand. You weren't there when I opened the class and explained to them what the three problems written on the board were. These are the three problems Albert Einstein could not solve. You worked two of them!"

Because George Danzig didn't hear anyone say, "It can't be done," he didn't know and was not affected by the negative words. What a God! Yield to Him. Whatever He has in mind to make of you is the best you can possibly be. Don't listen to the voices that may say, "It can't be done."

That's the power of the clay.

CHAPTER 2

THE POWER OF A CRUMB

Then Jesus went thence, and departed into the coasts of Tyre and Sidon. And, behold, a woman of Canaan came out of the same coasts, and cried unto Him, saying, Have mercy on me, O Lord, thou son of David; my daughter is grievously vexed with a devil. But He answered her not a word. And His disciples came and besought Him, saying, Send her away; for she crieth after us. But He answered and said, I am not sent but unto the lost sheep of the house of Israel. Then came she and worshiped Him, saying, Lord, help me. But He answered and said, It is not meet to take the children's bread, and to cast it to dogs. And she said, Truth, Lord: yet the dogs eat of the crumbs which fall from their masters' table. Then Jesus answered and said unto her, O woman, great is thy faith: be it unto thee even as thou wilt. And her daughter was made whole from that very hour (Matthew 15:21-28).

She was a woman in a society that subjugated those of her gender. She was a social outcast. If you piece together the

Gospel accounts, she was a Greek, a pagan—in addition to being a Canaanite, among those most hated by Jews. The Orthodox Jews still pray, "Lord, I thank thee I was not born a woman or a Gentile."

She was a mother—in fact, the mother of a desperately sick child. The Bible says the girl was "grievously vexed with a devil." But the mother had something she had not had in a long time. Hope. His name was Jesus.

"Great is Thy Faith" in Crumbs

He had departed into the coasts of Tyre and Sidon. Living at those same coasts was a woman of Canaan—miles from home—seeking a solution to her daughter's deadly dilemma. She knew He was a Jew. He knew she was a Gentile. But desperation made those things virtually insignificant. For, if by crossing established lines of society and religion her daughter might be helped, those lines would be crossed without hesitation. She cried out to Him, "Jesus, thou Son of David. Have mercy on me…"

It appears He ignored her. He answered her not a word. She persisted. Moffett's translation says, "She wailed after Him." The disciples ignored her. They tried to walk away, but she followed them. Finally, they turned to Jesus and said, "Master, send her away…" His response was to them, still not to her: "I am not sent but to the lost sheep of the house of Israel." It was as if He knew that if He acknowledged her He would have to help her. He could not leave her in her desperation; her need could not go unmet in His presence.

She must have been close enough and quiet enough at the moment to have heard His words to the disciples. The wailing stopped; the worship began. The Scripture says, "Then came she and worshiped Him...." Yet even that did not significantly change His response to her. He called the woman a dog! His seemingly offhand remark to her was, "It is not meet to take the children's bread, and to cast it to dogs" (Mt. 15:26; Mk. 7:27). But hope would not die and her answer was within reach. "Truth, Lord: yet the dogs eat of the crumbs which fall from their masters' table."

Jesus realized the tenacity of her faith, and the depth of her determination. He said to her, "O woman, great is thy faith: be it unto thee even as thou wilt." It wasn't often that He gave that kind of blanket answer. He didn't just say, "Be healed." He didn't even say, "Be whole." He said, in effect, "Woman, whatever you want—it is yours."

One Crumb Is Sufficient

So we see the power of a crumb. She wailed. She cried out to Him. She followed them wherever they went. They tried to avoid her; she stayed in their way. The words she finally heard from the disciples and then from Him were ultimately words of dismissal. He even called her a dog!

She should have been insulted. She could have gotten angry. Disappointment and doubt could have overwhelmed her. She could have gone away and become bitter and her daughter would never have become better. Instead, her faith soared. She heard more than what was spoken. You can often find hope between the lines of God, unspoken but not silent.

She was not asking for a meal with the children. She was not even seeking shared food with the servants in another room. She would have been satisfied with one crumb of truth, scattered and fallen to the floor under the Master's table, left for the dogs to lick up. She knew that even a crumb from His table could heal her daughter! She realized the power of a crumb! The dogs weren't allowed to come in while the master was present, only after he left the table. *One crumb from Your table—where You have been, not where You are—will suffice.*

She heard the talk of dogs and seized the crumb. She said, "This is my ticket in. I will ride into His favor on dogs, crumbs, and past presence. There is enough truth in that one word, 'dog,' to get what I need from Him."

She said to Him, "Truth, Lord. But since you made the allegory with dogs, can I remind you that even the dogs get a least the crumbs that fall from the master's table." What she was saying to Him was simple: "Lord, my faith in You is such that if one crumb is all I get, it is still sufficient to deliver and heal my daughter."

The word translated "dog" here actually means puppy. Have you ever had a puppy in your house? They come to you untrained and virtually uncontrollable and definitely demanding attention. Instead of being insulted, the Syrophoenician woman said, "That's okay. I'll be like a little puppy. I will claim nothing as a daughter of Abraham, because I am not one. But I am seeking the uncovenanted mercies of God. What I have asked of You, is nothing for You to do. All I need is a crumb from Your table."

If There Is Enough Power in one Crumb...

If there is enough power in one crumb to heal a sick daughter...

If there is enough power in one crumb from past presence to make the tormenting demons take flight...

If there is enough power in one crumb to cause Him to remain in His place and dispatch wholeness from Heaven...

If there is enough power in one crumb that an outcast Gentile woman received a "whatever-you-want-is-yours" response...

How much more power must there be in the whole loaf and permanent presence that belongs to the children of God today?

If He will do all that for a dog, with just a crumb, what is He willing and waiting to do for His children who gather around His table and have access to the Bread of Life?

We, today, as the Church of the living God, have more than crumbs because we are better than dogs. We are His "chosen generation, a royal priesthood, an holy nation, a peculiar people..." (1 Pet. 2:9).

If that outcast woman could seize on just the allusion to a dog, get a bulldog grip on a crumb, and bring a devil-chasing, divine healing experience into the life of her child—can we even comprehend what is available to us as the Spirit-born children of God?

As fathers put bread on the table so their children will not go hungry, so does our heavenly Father provide bread of healing for His children. If we can only comprehend the power that is in one crumb from the table of His provision, we will know that power in the Bread of Life is sufficient to walk the aisles of our lives and heal every sickness and disease, named and unnamed, which may befall the human condition.

There is power in a crumb to remove disease. There is power in a crumb to relieve every affliction. There is power in a crumb to drive out every spirit of depression. There is power in a crumb to break the bondage of every oppressing spirit. There is power in a crumb to lift every burden. He hears every prayer. He is able to heal every affliction—physical, mental, or spiritual. He is the Bread of Life and He is able! And there is power in just a crumb!

A Crumb Has Power Today

The Scripture tells us He is the same yesterday, today, and forever (see Heb. 13:8). What He has done He can do—and will do—again. The apostle declared that He is able to do exceeding, abundantly above all we ask or think (see Eph. 3:20).

When thoughts turn to eternity and our eternal reward, we often quote First Corinthians 2:9: "...Eye hath not seen, nor ear heard, neither have entered into the heart of man, the things which God hath prepared for them that love Him." We think of a street of gold. We thrill at the idea of walls of jasper, gates of pearl. A river of life—the throne of God. It is a city not made with hands. But if we really take an in-depth look at the Scripture, it actually refers to the saints in temporal life as well as eternal. As we traffic in time, troubled by its tests and trials, He says to us, "Your eyes haven't seen...your ears have not heard..."

I do not know the circumstances of your life as you read this. I cannot name your trial nor identify your physical illness, or the spirit that may trouble you. But I do know the promise that if all you can find is a crumb of faith, it will be enough to deliver you and your life.

Crumbs That Give Life

In the Old Testament, we find Elijah traveling with a word from the Lord to a house where He has promised provision. There the situation turns into quite an embarrassing one for all the players. First of all, a great prophet of God is to be depend-ent on a widow woman and, in effect, beg her assistance. When he speaks to her and asks for a cake to go with his water, it is her turn to be uncomfortable. She wants to take care of the prophet. She wants to be of service to the Lord in this unique way. However, she is without supplies and without money to secure them. She replies, "Master, all I have is a handful of meal—a few crumbs and a little oil. My plan for today is to use all I have and make a little cake for my son and me, and then we will die." All she has is crumbs (see 1 Kings 17:8-12).

Have you ever been there? A place where it seemed that the only faith you could dredge up was faith enough to die? The real test is whether you have faith enough to live.

Make God a Cake First

The prophet says to her, "Okay...here's a new plan. Take your oil...take your meal...and make me a cake first" (see

1 Kings 17:13). As brazenly demanding, as outlandish as it sounds—the woman somehow realizes that the things of God must always come first. The prophet is actually speaking what she already knows in her heart—that whatever happens, the care and feeding of the prophet should supersede the needs of her family and herself. She is about to discover the power of a crumb.

Take care of God's business first and He will always take care of the rest. "Seek ye first the kingdom of God and His righteousness..." (Mt. 6:33). The opposite scenario is also true: If you put God's Kingdom last and seek other things first you will find yourself without "all these things."

There is priority to be given to the word "first" in the Scripture. The prophet said, "Make me a cake first." Jesus said, "Seek first the kingdom..." Bring God "the firstfruits." He doesn't say "Bring Me *some* of the fruit." He specifically requires the first—not second, not third—not what's left. This principle can be demonstrated time and again in our lives. Your budget will work much better if you pay your tithes first and then the rest of your bills. God will honor your commitment to His desire for the first things. Only the firstborn, firstfruit, and first tenth have redemptive power over the rest.

The rest of the story of the widow and the prophet is familiar to many (see 1 Kings 17:14-16). She started with crumbs and some oil, barely enough for one cake for two people. But because she was willing to give what little she had to God, He took over the multiplication process. For as long as the drought lasted she never ran out of meal or oil. She didn't have to eat and die. She gave and lived. She understood the power of a crumb!

Hold On to a Crumb

If this kind of power is in just a crumb of faith, a crumb of commitment, a crumb of action in obedience to Him, then what could He do if we ever realize He is the Bread of Life and we have access not just to crumbs but to the entire loaf!?

God's message to Elijah was extraordinary: "You can touch this cake. You can touch these crumbs. But I am going to lead you from faith to faith until you graduate. You will remember all the things I have done. You will remember the crumbs from the barrel and see them parlayed into so much faith that you will reach up, without the

> ...WHAT COULD HE do if we ever realize He is the Bread of Life and we have access not just to crumbs but to the entire loaf!?

touch of hands, arrest a cloud in the sky, pull it over Israel, and hold onto that cloud until it becomes a rainstorm." Elijah's training on how to bring a rainstorm was learned from a lesson about a crumb. God said, "If you will be faithful over a few things..." (see Mt. 25:21,23).

The Bible says Lazarus, who sat at the gate of the rich man, ate crumbs. He kept holding on to those crumbs, without complaint. There's no record in the parable that Lazarus said, "God—look how blessed the rich man is—and look how poor I am!" He simply took his crumbs and held on until one day those crumbs bought him a chariot ride with the angels driving to the throne of God. The Bible says Lazarus was carried by angels but the rich man was simply buried (see Lk. 16:22). There is a difference.

Remember this: There are times when we want a miracle but God wants us to have faith.

The Syrophenician woman's attitude—her ability to find a crumb of faith in the truth spoken to her—was power to hold on. It made Jesus say, "Great is thy faith" (Mt. 15:28).

When Daniel found himself thrown in a den of lions, he may have thought God would miraculously deliver him by killing all the lions. Likewise, the young Hebrew men in the fiery furnace would have welcomed a miracle of deliverance. God, however, was looking for faith. Faith that stopped the mouths of the lions. Faith that brought safety to a fiery furnace.

There are times in our lives when we seek deliverance— miraculous, simple deliverance. But God wants us to have faith—faith enough to hold on. Holding on is a difficult thing to do. But holding on does not, by definition, mean being miserable. There are times when you have to persevere. Times when you have to keep knocking on the door.

It has been said, "When the going gets tough, the tough get going." Sometimes staying is what God is seeking. The sky is black. Hold on. The way is rough. Hold on. The desert is scorching. Hold on. The wilderness is wearying. Hold on. There is no way out. Hold on. If you seem to be looking up through the bottom, hold on. If you're in a fiery furnace, hold on. If you have just a crumb, hold on. He is on His way!

Will God Find a Crumb of Faith

The question in Luke 18:8—"When the Son of man cometh shall He find faith on the earth?"—is often quoted. A simple word study will show the faith He is seeking here is not on the earth as much as in the Church, the Body of Christ. A closer look at the parable that precedes this Scripture shows us the kind of faith for which He is looking (see Lk. 18:1-7). It is the story of a widow who went to a judge, knocked on his door, and said, "Avenge me of my adversary." The judge said, "I will not." The next day, another knock—the same woman, the same demand, the same response. Again and again. Finally the judge grew exasperated and said, "Okay! Enough is enough. I do not fear God; I do not fear you. However, because you will not leave me alone, because you keep coming back to me despite my denial of your request, I am going to give you what you have asked for."

Suddenly we see that the real question is: "When the Son of man comes, will He find *persevering* faith?" It is the power of a crumb—a crumb that you hold onto until the whole loaf is in your hands. He will be looking for faith that has been tried by the delay of deliverance. When we pray and ask God for something, we think He ought to have sent the answer to us yesterday. However, we must always remember God does not operate on our timetable.

Your Crumbs Are Part of the Plan

Abraham is called the "Father of the faithful." He never owned an acre of real estate, except the burial ground where he and his beloved wife were buried. He lived one hundred years, tenaciously holding onto a promise that he never saw fulfilled in his lifetime. He had to comprehend that he was part of the eternal purpose of God. You and I must grasp the same. I am just one little cog in the wheel; you are just one piece of the puzzle. However, we are vital to the completion and fulfill-ment of His eternal will and plan.

God said, "In thee shall all nations of the world be blessed. You will be as the sands of the seashore and the stars in the sky" (see Gen. 22:17-18), but Abraham never saw it in his lifetime. God said, "Get up and walk up and down the length and breadth of the land. It is all yours. From the great river of Egypt to the River Euphrates—claim it as your own" (see Gen. 13:14-18). Abraham never inherited it. But he recognized by faith that he was just one segment of the eternal purpose of God. The graves at Hebron were his crumbs. Abraham believed in the power of a crumb. His main inheritance was to be a blessing to others. His crumb joined the sands of earth to the stars of Heaven.

So the World Can See

Sometimes in the situations of our own lives, we wonder, *God, why won't You deliver me from this? Why won't You bring me out of this situation? Why don't You do something?!* If we can ever comprehend that we are part of the eternal pur-pose of God, which is so much more than what we can see and feel, if we can ever realize the power of a crumb—we will be forever changed.

God has some modern-day Jobs around. There are countless individuals among us that are victims of situations beyond their control. There are losses they suffer, heart-breaks they endure for no reason at all except to prove to the world that the God of Job is alive and working in our world today. I believe there are people among us, afflicted and tried in all circumstances of life, so the world can see "epistles known and read of all men" (see 2 Cor. 3:2). There are people who will never read the Bible story of Job but who will watch the lives of men and women walking with God through life's situations and know He is God.

In Hebrews 11 we read what some have called the parade of conquerors, the Arlington Cemetery of the Old Testament. They were individuals like you and me. They were cut from the same bolt of human cloth. They were ex-harlots, and former murderers, and redeemed drunkards. Everyone listed there, when studied closely, had some proverbial skeletons in their closets. They had hang-ups. They had tragedies. They had irrevocable mistakes in their past behaviors. They became trophies of grace because they discovered the power of a crumb of faith, a crumb of effort, and a crumb of hope.

Some people perceive God as some kind of spiritual heavenly gestapo, the traffic sergeant of the sky; the lightning as His nightstick of power; the evening star as His badge of authority; the thunder as His growl of rage. From His lofty observatory He asks, "Are you folks enjoying life?" If the answer is yes, His response is, "Don't you know you have to be miserable to be holy?" This picture of our heavenly Father is just not so. As Christians we still face the trials and traumas of life, encountering difficulties along our life's way, but we have a Savior. We still are faced with illness and disease, but we have a Healer. Whether He chooses to heal us temporarily in the moments of this life, or eternally by delivering us past death, we still have a Healer. We have troubles that come our way but we have a God who knows exactly where we are and is able to deliver us. Job said, "He knoweth the way that I take..." (Job 23:10).

Sharing Crumbs With Your Children

Some people reading this book are fourth generation Spirit-filled believers. You have been in the land four generations and some of you have Spirit-filled great-great-grandparents. I wonder if there are parents reading this who are ready to hold onto God until their children see the old-time power. The Syrophenician woman held on until she had an experience from God that could transfer to her daughter.

Deuteronomy 4:25 says, "After you've been in the land, and your children have children, you are going to corrupt yourself with many idols" (author's translation). Moffett's translation says, "If you are not careful, after you have been in the land four generations you are going to lose your freshness."

The younger generations today are grievously vexed. They are troubled. They are fearful. They are upset. They are tired of phonies. They are not attracted to the artificial. They are seeking real people and real experiences. If they do not find this in the Church, where will they find it?

While I am committed to excellence, I fear professionalism. I fear professional worship. I fear professional singing. I fear professional prayer. I fear professional preaching. "Whatsoever ye do, do it heartily, as unto the Lord" (Col. 3:23a). Professionalism can be deadly when it removes from the equation the reason for the worship—it's for the Worshiped One, not the worshiper.

In the Old Testament, the Lord instructed Moses to make anointing oil, which required five ingredients: pure myrrh, sweet cinnamon, sweet calamus, cassia, and olive oil (see Ex.

30:23-25). He told him how to grind the spices, how to formulate the perfume, and how to add in the oil. He then gave very specific guidelines as to where it was to be used: on the lamp stand, the table, the laver, the altar. They were to anoint everything— except themselves. It was not to be used on flesh. In fact, God's instruction included a warning: "If you use it on flesh, you will be cut off" (see Ex. 30:32-33). The oil was for the glory of God, not for sensual appreciation.

Sing all you want to sing, but do it to the glory of God. Dance all you want to dance, but do it to the glory of God. Shout all you want to shout, but not to be sensuous, not just to exhibit some outward measure of holiness. That is hypocrisy at its worst. For the promise of God is, "I will cut you off." The use of holy oil and the anointing of the Holy Spirit is to the glory of God and to His glory alone. "They that worship Him must worship Him in spirit and in truth" (Jn. 4:24b). Sensuous worship is a fearful thing. We must sing to the glory of God. We must preach to the glory of God. We must worship Him and Him alone. Honor can be given to man, but glory belongs to God alone.

The Bible says God judged Eli, not for his sin, but for the iniquity he knew—the sins of his sons. He knew what his children were doing. As a priest, he knew what they were doing was wrong before God. They were taking the best and he was getting fat on it. He may have said, "God, I am not guilty of that. I did not do it." His excuse may have been, "Well, it's a new generation... " But the fact is God held him responsible for knowing what his children were doing.

Our children need to see a real Spirit-filled experience lived and acted in the Church, in the pulpit, and in our homes. Fathers need to be the high priests of their homes and lead in family devotion and reading the Word. A father may not be able to control what his children do, but he can decide whether to condone or ignore it, or address and correct it. I've seen parents who are secretly glad to see their children taking "freedoms" they themselves did not experience. I've known parents whose children have grown up to be successful businessmen and women of the world, yet not walk with the Lord.

We are only one generation from extinction. Only one generation, ignoring and distorting the basic truths of any religious enterprise, can forever alter its own course. I want my children, my grandchildren, and my great-grandchildren to know and experience firsthand the power of God in their lives. I want them to love His truth. I want to give them the whole loaf. I want them to know they are children of promise, not dogs. I want them to be sanctified by believing parents. I want them to see, feel, experience, and live apostolic, pentecostal fire.

We can make issues of non-issues and pretty soon we have discussed away and rationalized everything that has brought us biblical distinctiveness. However, the Lord set some distinctives for the children of Israel, although He didn't always give an explanation. He said, "Don't mix diverse seeds."[1] He said, 'Don't plow an ox and an ass together."[2] Why? I don't know. He said, "Don't mix fabrics—linen and wool."[3] Why? There are just some separations to be made. He said, "...be ye separate" (2 Cor. 6:17a).

We cannot begin to replace God's periods with our own question marks. We cannot put a gate where God has placed a fence, nor a fence where He has established a gate. There are some things that simply must be left alone.

The Syrophenician woman held on until her daughter had a delivering experience and saw the glory of God in her own life. We cannot become satisfied with what we have and let our children go to the devil. We cannot raise our children for hell.

One Man and a Crumb

All Abraham had was a crumb. According to Jewish folklore, Abraham's father, Terah, was an idol-maker. Tradition says he worshiped many false gods. As Abraham was walking through his father's shop of idolatry one day, he heard a voice. Suddenly, without a Bible, without a pastor, without saints to pat him on the back and carry him on a feather pillow when he didn't come to church, he heard a voice. "Abram. Get thee out from among thy kindred to a land I will show thee" (see Gen. 12:1).

He couldn't run down to the local Texaco station and check a roadmap. He didn't have Rand McNally on a laptop computer; a NavStar system was not available to him. He didn't know where he was going or how long it would take to get there. He simply knew he had a word from the Lord God of Israel. And...he didn't hear the voice again for many years. On the basis of that one crumb, he literally marched off the map. He went forth not knowing where he was going but knowing Who he was following. He did it with the power of a crumb.

The Bible says Abraham believed God and it was counted unto him for righteousness (see Gen. 15:6). From that one man whom the Lord took from the Euphrates River, from Ur of the Chaldees, a place whose name means the "flames of destruction, fire, and light."—from that one man God raised up one nation: Israel. From that one nation, God took one tribe: the tribe of Judah. From that one tribe, God took one lineage: the lineage of David. From that one lineage, God brought forth one Man whose blood atones for the sins of the world, who is now exalted on the right hand of God and ever maketh intercession for the saints. You can trace it all back to a man who took hold of a crumb and held on until it became the Bread of Life.

Out With the Power

Blessing is God flowing into our lives. Power is God flowing out from us. In His encounter with the woman with the issue of blood, we read that Jesus said, "I felt virtue pass from Me" (see Lk. 8:46). Too often today, we want blessing but we don't want the power to flow out. We want it to come in like a mighty flood but we are not willing to let it flow out. Jesus said, "Ye shall receive power, after that the Holy Ghost is come upon you..." (Acts 1:8). A world in crisis needs a Church in revival.

Jesus said, "If you have faith as of a grain of mustard seed, you can say to this mountain, 'Be thou removed...' " We usually think that means if you have a little bit of faith, God will do something. I personally think it means that you can take a little seed—a crumb of faith—drop it into an impossible situation, cover it up, and trust it. And, before the story ends, it will grow through every obstacle, knock rocks apart, and come popping out. Trust the process of the seed.

I cannot know the circumstances of each reader's life. However, I can challenge you, whatever your circumstance, to drop one seed of faith into it. Be patient. Wait on the Lord. And before the story is told, victory will be yours.

The Whole Loaf

We are in an age of crisis. We need to be a people that move in by faith and, having held the crumb, hold on by faith to claim the whole loaf—the children's bread. I don't want someone from the outside to come in and seize a crumb and do more than we are doing with the whole loaf. I've heard it said that if we fail God, He will raise up another people. But I don't think He wants to do that. And I do not want Him to have to do that.

We have His Spirit, we have His Word, we have His name, we have thousands of angels at our disposal—it is the whole loaf. John tried to number the angels and gave up the count. He said in the Book of Revelation, "I saw ten thousand and ten thousand and thousands of thousands." The Bible says, "...the angels of the Lord encamp around them that fear him." So let's figure that equation. Ten thousand multiplied by ten thousand and then thousands (which is more than one, at least two to be plural) and thousands (plural again). Sooner or later when you multiply ten thousand times ten thousand and then that by two thousand once and again, the number reaches somewhere around four hundred trillion. They are encamping around us. They are ministering spirits sent to minister to the heirs of salvation. We have been given the whole loaf.

The Syrophoenician mother claimed two words—*truth* and *dogs*. With those two words, a devil was cast out from her

MORE POWER TO YOU

daughter and the girl was restored to her right mind. "What manner of love the Father hath bestowed upon us, that we should be called the sons of God...Beloved, now are we the sons of God..." (1 Jn. 3:1-2).

The power of a crumb. Look what the woman did with the little faith she had. "Truth, Master. But the puppies get the crumbs." We have been given more than crumbs because we are better than dogs. The children's portion is the whole loaf!

Endnotes

1. See Deuteronomy 22:9.
2. See Deuteronomy 22:10.
3. See Deuteronomy 22:11.

CHAPTER 3

THE POWER OF HIS GLORY

In the year that king Uzziah died I saw also the Lord sitting upon a throne, high and lifted up, and His train filled the temple. Above it stood the seraphim: each one had six wings; with twain he covered his face, and with twain he covered his feet, and with twain he did fly. And one cried unto another, and said, Holy, holy, holy, is the Lord of hosts: the whole earth is full of His glory. And the posts of the door moved at the voice of him that cried, and the house was filled with smoke. Then said I, Woe is me! for I am undone; because I am a man of unclean lips, and I dwell in the midst of a people of unclean lips: for mine eyes have seen the King, the Lord of hosts. (Isaiah 6:1-5).

In the sixth chapter of Isaiah we read, "In the year that king Uzziah died I saw *also* the Lord..." When King Uzziah's earthly throne of prominence and strength was emptied, Isaiah lifted his eyes above that earthly throne to see *also* another throne that is never empty. So often God must empty one throne in order to focus our human attention on the throne of the ascended One that is always filled. There is a release of power that exists in the presence of the raw unfiltered glory of God. Is it then possible to be in His presence and not comprehend His glory?

The Question of Perception

In the passage cited, the seraphim said, "The whole earth is full of His glory." They saw something of which humanity was not aware. I can honestly say I have never seen in totality the whole Church full of His glory. How then can the whole earth be full of His glory? It is a question of perception. The seraphim lived in the glory. Consequently, when they opened their eyes and looked at earth, they only saw the earth through the glory.

They saw the glory before problems. They saw the glory before sin. They saw the glory before failure. They could say, "From where we're standing, the whole earth is full of the glory of God." We are not interested in the possibilities of defeat; they do not exist where we are. The battlefield bulletins of victory have already been printed. Jesus said, "Upon this rock I will build My church; and the gates of hell shall not prevail against it" (Mt. 16:18b).

"For the earth shall be full with the knowledge of the Lord as the waters cover the sea." What is your perspective? In the glory—through the glory—I see signs, wonders, miracles. I see an outpouring such as we have never seen before! He said, "I will pour out My spirit upon all flesh..." (Joel 2:28b).

Have you ever perceived His glory? Nothing is going to happen until we see things from God's perspective. Whenever

Moses saw the backside of the glory, he was secluded in a rock. When Paul saw the glory, he was knocked off his donkey. When John saw the glory, he fell on his face. Regardless of what claims we make, I doubt if many of us have truly seen the full glory of God. When the full, unveiled glory of God is present, you are literally knocked from your standing position. That is the kind of glory that is going to fill the Church, and fill the earth. It is the knowledge of the glory of God. You have to see it from God's vantage point, and know it from God's vantage point.

Holy, Holy, Holy

The only time the seraphim are mentioned in the Scripture is in this passage of Isaiah 6. The word *seraphim* means "shiny, fiery ones." They did not have inherent glory; they were reflections of the fiery, shiny glory of God. They reflected Him. In Isaiah's vision, there were apparently at least two of them, flying around the throne of God. They each had six wings: two covered their feet, two their face, and with two they "did fly." And they said, "Holy, holy, holy."

Some might speculate they were making this utterance to God. Personally, I think they may have been speaking to themselves, reminding each other of the holiness that is the presence of God. As far as we know, that one word was their total vocabulary. They were gripped by the presence of a holy, awesome, powerful, majestic God. They, too, saw Him high and lifted up. They saw the King of all the earth, His glory and His train filling the temple.

The Hebrew language does not have superlatives as the English language does. There is no *highest, greatest, lowest,* or *sweetest.* To express their superlatives the Jews repeat the same word. The highest superlative in that language is a word used three times. For instance, Jesus probably spoke Aramaic. Consequently, He would say "Verily, verily," to emphasize a point.

Instead of being able to say, "This is the greatest, of the greatest, of the greatest of God," they said, "Holy, holy," to the highest superlative, "Holy." That was the highest degree of language. Repeatedly spoken it doubled and tripled the intensity of its meaning.

We cannot look at God through our problems. We must look at our problems through God. "Is the earth in bad shape, seraphim?"

"Holy."

"Isn't there a lot of sin down there?"

"Holy."

"Don't you see all those failures of mankind?"

"Holy!"

Their response was basically: "From where we're standing, all we can see is revival—the earth full of His glory." So why then should we get hung up on anything else?

God must not ever tire of hearing that word ascribed to Himself. They were crying "holy" in Isaiah. Then in the New Testament we find the same task being performed in Revelation 4:8. (In Revelation they are not called seraphim, but in all probability it may be the same creatures.) "Holy, holy, holy." The time from Isaiah to the writing of Revelation was nearly a thousand years. God was still on His throne and accepting that adoration and praise, "Holy, holy, holy."

Using Your Wings of Worship to Move the Presence of God

When the seraphim cried, "Holy, holy, holy" to one another, the pillars began to move and the throne room was filled with smoke. Where was the smoke coming from? Verse 6 identifies the source. An altar was burning. Worship and adoration were being offered and from this altar smoke was filling the air. What provoked it to fill the room rather than hover over the altar? The voice of the angels, the seraphim.

How God loves worship! How He manifests His glory in the presence of worship! What power there is in His glory! They simply said that one word for a thousand years; they are still saying it today. "Holy, holy, holy." It was to the highest degree. Worship should be uncomplicated and simple, enduring through the ages.

There is a significant difference in the presence of God and the manifest presence of God. The presence of God is always here. But if you want the presence of God to be manifest and to move, begin worshiping. Find your wings! Let's get the smoke stirred up! "Holy! Holy! Holy!" I want the manifest presence of God. I know it is here. I want it to move. The moving of those seraphim wings is indicative of worship.

Nothing is going to move until worship begins. Notice I didn't say *noise*, I said *worship*. The foundations didn't rumble, the doorposts didn't move until the worship began. God revels in worship. He inhabits the praise of His people. We need that kind of worship.

Paul said we are the pillar and ground of truth (see 1 Tim. 3:15). We are the pillar and ground—the spirit and truth. Spirit is supported by truth; truth is supported by Spirit. All of this is built around a knowledge of the all-inspiring holiness of God. The purpose of foundational worship is to recognize, not mechanically but from your heart, that you are in the presence of the King of the universe. You cannot take it for granted. You are awestruck, smitten by it. It is not just "regular service," because there is nothing regular about it. When Jesus is present, things move.

Paul and Silas began worshiping in the literal foundation— or dungeon—of the Philippian jail. It rose from the foundation to God's throne, the citadel of praise. Worship always rises. Although it began on earth, it fell ultimately on the ears of God. Subsequently, He ordered an earthquake angel to report for duty. Worship rose from the foundation of human lips to the highest Heaven and then its power descended into the depths of the earth until it affected under the earth, on the earth, and in the heavens. That is the power of worship.

Worship in Spirit and Truth

There is a unique Scripture in Zephaniah 1:9. The Lord said, "I'm going to get you for jumping over a threshold" (author's translation). I read that a few years ago and wondered, "Now, God, what difference does that make? Why would You want to punish them for jumping over a threshold? What's wrong with that?"

Here's the proverbial "rest of the story." When the ark was captured by the Philistines, the head of their idol Dagon broke off in the threshold. The idol literally fell on his face in the presence of the glory of the ark. The Bible says that from that day on the Philistines would not walk over that threshold; they'd jump over it. To the Philistines it was a means of acknowledging the power of the God of Israel, who had destroyed their god. Evidently the Hebrews thought that was cute, so they decided to imitate the action.

However, God doesn't want mechanical worship. He doesn't want the automatic reflex kind of activity. He doesn't want us to do what we do in worship because someone else does it that way. He wants the kind of worship that proceeds from our heart, in spirit and in truth, because we love Him and because He is "Holy! Holy! Holy!" Turn the threshold of your mechanical worship over and it will read "Made in Philistia by Philistines." He is not interested in mechanical, fleshly, Pentecostal, or charismatic bunny hops. He wants spirit and truth.

The Presence of Jesus

In the Gospels we find the story of Jesus coming to the country of the Gadarenes. He was met there by a man possessed with many devils. According to Mark's account, "When he saw Jesus afar off, he ran and worshiped Him" (Mk. 5:6). This man did not see Jesus clearly enough to recognize him. He had not even heard Jesus speak. Yet when Jesus hit the shore, the demons in this man started doing somersaults and he knew something was different. The presence of Jesus—the promise of deliverance—drew the man to Him. Oh, the power of His glory! When Jesus showed up, the devils were disturbed, and had to leave the man they had tormented so unmercifully. Demons are sensitive to His presence. I would hate to think that fallen angels would be more sensitive to His presence than we are.

The power of His glory is such that when the demoniac found Himself in the presence of Jesus, the demons demanded their freedom. When we get in the presence of God in His glory, God will manifest Himself. And when God shows up there are miracles, signs, and wonders!

When the presence of God and His glory manifests itself, anything can happen because healing is in this smoke. Worship attracts the presence of a holy God and everything that He is. Yet there is a difference between worship and praise. All you must do to praise the Lord is breathe. The Psalmist said, "Let everything that has breath praise the Lord" (Ps. 150:6). But to worship Him, you must know Him. You must move beyond the dimension of praise, which is the surface of something deeper. Worship takes you into the depths—deep to the foundations, to the moving of the pillars, the manifestation of His glory and His power and His presence.

Sometimes in the presence of Jesus and His glory, perspective and perception change. The old song "Turn Your Eyes Upon Jesus" says, "And the things of earth will grow strangely dim in the light of His glory and grace." For instance, in John's account, Simon Peter was comfortably naked with the others in the boat. Yet when Jesus showed up, he was uncomfortable as he was and jumped into

WORSHIP TAKES YOU into the depths...of His glory and His power and His presence.

the water. When Jesus shows up, a lot of things will take care of themselves. All Peter's self-doubt and loathing, his fears and failures, mattered little at that moment. In the presence of Jesus, everything was made right.

The Scriptures call us as Christians to a separated lifestyle. But we also need a manifestation of the supernatural in our churches. To simply enforce a raw code of ethics is not enough; people can join any professional association to adhere to some rules. But when Jesus shows up, their lives will be changed, and they will desire to come back for more of His presence.

According to Revelation 6:16-17, you come into His presence before you come to His person: "And said to the mountains and rocks, Fall on us, and hide us from the face [or presence] of Him that sitteth on the throne, and from the wrath of the Lamb: for the great day of His wrath is come; and who shall be able to stand?" If we can get people into the presence of God, we can then lead them to a full knowledge of the person of God. His presence will open them to a revelation of truth.

Sitting on the Mercy Seat

The presence of God will remove you from sitting on the judgment seat. In chapter 5, Isaiah declared six times, "Woe unto them..." Six is the number of man; it is a judgmental number. Seven is the number of God. When Isaiah saw the Lord and envisioned the presence and power of His glory, his tune changed. Read what he said then: "Woe is me." Like the old spiritual song says, "It's not my brother, not my sister, but it's me, oh Lord!"

We must understand in this dispensation, God's favorite seat is the mercy seat. In the Old Testament tabernacle and temple, God lived in a three-room house. His living room had one piece of furniture—a love seat called "the mercy seat."

Jesus said, "He that overcometh and sits down with Me in My throne as I overcame and sat down in My Father's throne" (see Rev. 3:21). Pardon my colloquialism, but if you are going to sit in Jesus' lap today, you'll be sitting on the throne of mercy. Someday He will sit on the throne of judgment, but He's not there today. If you are sitting in a seat or throne of judgment, you are not sitting with Jesus. You are not where you are supposed to be.

"I don't like the way my preacher preaches." Get off your judgment seat.

"I don't like the way the singer sings." Get off your judgment seat.

When you are in the presence of God, all you can see is the glory of God. It blinds you to all else but Him. When God shows up, all things are placed in the right perspective. You'd be surprised how good your pastor is when you get in the presence and the power of His glory.

Ruined by the Glory

So what, or Who, did Isaiah see in Isaiah 6? According to John, "These things said Isaiah, when he saw His [Jesus'] glory, and spake of Him" (Jn. 12:41).

Jesus of the New Testament was Jehovah of the Old Testament. "And the Word was made flesh and dwelt among us, (and we beheld His glory, the glory as of the only begotten of the Father)..." (Jn. 1:14). When did Isaiah see the glory of Jesus? When Isaiah saw that One on the throne, he saw the same One who came in flesh as the Son of God. John could say, "Isaiah saw the glory of Jesus..." (Jn. 12:41). If we could only get a glimpse of the glory—and the power of that glory!

Isaiah saw it in future tense; we see it in present tense. He saw it in symbol; we see it in substance. "Woe is me," Isaiah said, "when I see what God is and who I am." He said, "I am undone." I like the NIV version of that passage. It says, "I am ruined." The presence of the glory will ruin you for anything else. Once you get a taste of this, you are ruined. You may as well dive off and get in it, because you are ruined for anything less. Prodigal, you can drift away from this, but when you think about the glory of your Father's house, you'll come to yourself and say, "If I can just get back to my Father...if I can only get back to His glory..."

You can join anything you want to join, but you'll still be ruined. You can drift as far away as you want to drift, but once you've tasted of this, you're ruined for any other brand. Once you have seen Him high and lifted up, and there's smoke all over the place, you will never be satisfied with less.

On the day of Pentecost, the crowd said, "These men are drunk..." (see Acts 2:13). How long has it been since you've been accused of being drunk on your brand of religion? David said, "I want to see your power and glory as I have seen Thee in the sanctuary."[1] He said, "I'm not asking for anything new, but I want this generation to see what I've seen."

Every generation must see, feel, and experience the presence for themselves. You cannot live on stories from the past. Twice in my lifetime—and only twice—have I seen a visible manifestation of the glory cloud. Once years ago in South America, in a great convention where several thousand people were worshiping and praising God, we looked to the back of the tabernacle and saw a blue cloud hovering over part of the congregation. As it moved over the people, it was as if everyone under it was being rained on. People fell, people were baptized in the Holy Ghost, people were healed. We stood on the platform awestricken as we watched the cloud of glory traverse the meeting place. We beheld the literal moving of the glory cloud!

The campground in Louisiana where I currently maintain an office and a residence is home to one of the longest-running old-fashioned camp meetings in North America. Several years ago in our Tabernacle building on the campground, during a camp meeting service, I again saw a visible manifestation of a glory cloud.

Isaiah said, "I'm caught between me and the glory and I'm ruined." That is what must happen to us. We must experience the power of His glory. We must find the place where we bask in the glory! Imperative for everyone is a little carpet time. How long has it been since you've been slain and prostrate before the Lord, feeling His presence and His power so strongly you could not stand up or walk? I am not talking about something that only happens in your flesh—but something in the supernatural, something in your spirit that evokes a true hunger for God and His presence. God, give us a return to hunger! Let us experience the power of your glory! The glory changes the terrain!

My Lips Burn With Praise

Isaiah said, "When I look at me in the light of Him, I am silenced in His presence. My lips can utter nothing but praise." You don't look at Him in the light of you; you look at you in the light of Him. It's always us in the light of Him. I can hear Isaiah, "I can't worship with them; my lips and my being stains what I would say. I am simply awestruck at His glory."

Notice now some symbolism in this passage from Isaiah 6. The altar is burning. Was it perhaps the altar of incense? One of the seraphim comes, takes a tong, and picks up a live coal. I used to preach a sermon entitled "Too Hot for Angels to Handle." The angels couldn't touch the coal with their hands or their wings; they had to have tongs to transport the fiery coal. Speaking of the Holy Ghost being sent from Heaven, Peter noted that it was something the angels "desire to look into" (1 Pet. 1:12).

The coal from the altar was too hot to be handled. The power of the glory of His presence was too hot for angels to handle! But equipped with the tongs, the angel was able to place the coal on human lips. There is no mention of it burning Isaiah; only that as it touched his lips and tongue, his tongue was loosed. When he received the touch of fire, in the presence of the awe-inspiring God, his tongue was loosed. Though it may be too hot for angels to handle, like Isaiah of old, pour it on me! It fits human lips.

In my personal study, I find only one altar in Heaven—the altar of incense, which is the altar of praise, in Revelation 8:3. Praise will continue through eternity. The brazen altar will not be there. There will be no need for a brazen altar of blood sacrifices in the holy city, because our sacrifice will be forever on the Throne. We will need the incense of praise forever and forever. "Holy! Holy! Holy!" A thousand years from now—"Holy!" A million years from now—"Holy!" "Worthy is the Lamb that was slain!" "Holy! Holy! Holy!"

Real holiness forces you to look at yourself. Isaiah said, "Woe is me." It makes you look inward. The best way in the world to preach holiness is with the way you practice it. If you have holiness without love, it is not God's kind of holiness. If you have love without holiness, it is not God's kind of love.

"Yes, but look what everybody else is doing."

Just because somebody else is practicing something, doesn't make it right. We are called to be a holy people. We can sing together, "Holy, holy, holy..." The question is, do our lips and spirit burn with the sense of His awesome presence, or is it just empty echoing words spoken by rote? When we truly seek God in His holiness, it is self-revelatory. We see ourselves and are driven to worship and adoration. We are awestricken, shaken from the foundation to the pillars. Every now and then we must experience a personal encounter with the power of His glory and with the holiness of God.

Can you imagine that the infinite God will become intimate with man in an act of worship? This kind of worship is not a parade of pageantry; it is a march of intimacy.

Breathing the Power Through the Word

It is awesome to think the holy God is omnipresent. He is not just on His throne; He is as close as my breath.

The Word is the creative breath of God. "All scripture is given by inspiration" (2 Tim. 3:16a). *Inspiration* means "God breathed." We must be sensitive to His breath. Too often we respond to the rushing wind and are not sensitive to His breath. Too often we get excited with singing and outward demonstration. Yet there is more concentrated power of God present when the Word is preached than any other time. Do I have the text to prove that? "For I am not ashamed of the gospel of Christ: for it is the power of God" (Rom. 1:16a). It doesn't say singing is the power, though I like to sing the power down. It doesn't say praying, though I like to pray in the Spirit. There is simply more of the power of God present when the Word is preached. The glory of His presence is in His Word, the Word that is forever settled in Heaven (see Ps. 119:89).

His Glory Is Always Available

Recall with me the story of the father of John the Baptist, Zacharias. We can read about him in Luke chapters 1 and 2. Only the high priest could go in the Holiest of Holies. Once a year a rope was tied around the leg of the high priest. Fearfully and with much wonder, he went in to that Holiest of Holies. He did not enter it boldly, as we can today, because at that time the veil was not yet rent. There were hundreds of priests that could go in to the holy place, where the incense, the bread, and the candlestick were located; and they were chosen by lot for this once-in-a-lifetime experience. On one particular day, the lot fell on Zacharias. It would be his only time to go into the presence of Almighty God. But today, we don't have to wait in line for our turn. His glory, through Christ, is always available.

Worthy Is the Lamb

As you look at yourself in the light of His holiness, perhaps the Holy Spirit is convicting you of something in your life that is not quite right. The greatest glory of God is the grace of God. It is found in His presence. His throne is a throne of grace. As I said earlier in this chapter, His favorite seat is the mercy seat. It is good and proper to be smitten of sin. Yet that cannot be the end of it. When we sin and are smitten by our guilt, we must find a place of repentance and forgiveness that brings understanding of God's grace.

The ancient Puritans used to lick the floor of their dirty cabins to do penance. I have personally seen men in foreign countries carry crosses as also an act of penance. We don't have to do any of those things. The Holy Spirit does not just convict of sin and leave us; He convicts us unto righteousness. Do you feel like Isaiah? "I'm undone; I'm unclean." That does not have to be the end of your story.

In the Old Testament, a man who had sinned was obligated to bring a sheep or lamb to the priests at the tabernacle to offer as a sacrifice. There were no other specifications given that the man had to personally adhere to other than that he present the lamb to the priest. However, there were detailed instructions for the lamb. The priest never looked at the man; he looked at the lamb. Was the animal diseased? Did it have all his faculties? Was it lame in any way? Was it a perfect lamb?

The priest could say, "Your presence here, man, tells me you are guilty. The only other thing I need to see is the lamb. If the lamb is worthy to be offered, then you are accepted." So it is with us. There is nothing we can do except leave ourselves to the mercy and grace of the spotless Lamb of God, slain from the foundation.

That Lamb of God was an acceptable sacrifice. Because He was accepted, I am accepted in the Beloved. He is my righteousness, He is my Savior, He is my King! By nothing I did have my sins been remitted. Jesus paid it all! I want the power of His glory.

I want His smoke to fill the temple. I want the manifest glory. We must see ourselves in the light of His glory. Oh, God! I'm ruined! I have unclean lips, so touch me with that live coal, and set me free again! I must see myself first. Repentance must come. Worship must be born. Then we can see as He sees—through the power of His glory! Then we can see as the seraphim saw—through the power of His glory!

I invite you to enter His presence and experience the power of His glory!

Endnote

1. See Psalms 63:2.

CHAPTER 4

THE POWER OF HIS NAME

Now Peter and John went up together into the temple at the hour of prayer, being the ninth hour. And a certain man lame from his mother's womb was carried, whom they laid daily at the gate of the temple which is called Beautiful, to ask alms of them that entered into the temple; who seeing Peter and John about to go into the temple asked an alms. And Peter, fastening his eyes upon him with John, said, Look on us. And he gave heed unto them, expecting to receive something of them. Then Peter said, Silver and gold have I none; but such as I have give I thee: In the name of Jesus Christ of Nazareth rise up and walk. And he took him by the right hand, and lifted him up: and immediately his feet and ankle bones received strength. And he leaping up stood, and walked, and entered with them into the temple, walking, and leaping, and praising God. And all the people saw him walking and praising God: and they knew that it was he which sat for alms at the Beautiful gate of the temple: and they were filled with wonder and amazement at that which had happened unto him. And as the lame man which was healed held Peter and John, all the people ran together unto them in the porch that is called Solomon's, greatly wondering (Acts 3:1-11).

And His name through faith in His name hath made this man strong, whom ye see and know: yea, the faith which is by him hath given Him this perfect soundness in the presence of you all (Acts 3:16).

And when they had set them in the midst, they asked, By what power, or by what name, have ye done this? (Acts 4:7)

But that it spread no further among the people, let us straitly threaten them, that they speak henceforth to no man in this name (Acts 4:17).

Included in God's Word are four Books that share the life stories of Jesus, who came to save the lost. Following these Gospels are the epistles—love letters and corrections to a Church already saved by His grace. And what we find in between is the powerhouse Scripture; the yellow pages of the New Testament—the Book of Acts. Here is the where and how of the New Testament Church—built on and established by the power of the name of Jesus. The name of Jesus is mentioned 67 times in the Book of Acts, not to mention the additional derivative or reference usages. There is power in the name of Jesus and the Book of Acts is an extensive documentation of that name.

Through Faith in His Name

It was through the power of the name of Jesus that the lame man lying at the temple was healed. At the words of Peter, "In the name of Jesus Christ of Nazareth rise up and walk," the man stood up. According to the scriptural account, "Immediately his feet and ankle bones received strength. And he leaping up stood, and walked, and entered with them into the temple, walking, and leaping, and praising God."

The lame man had lain at the gate of the temple for years. He had heard people speak of its awe-inspiring splendor; yet the Law forbade him entry because of his physical limitations. Miraculously, the name of Jesus opened doors the Law had barred shut. He gained admittance by the power of His name!

When questioned about the incident, Peter reiterated the lame man's story: "His [Jesus'] name through faith in His name hath made this man strong" (Acts 3:16a). In Acts chapter 4, when Peter was brought before the rulers, elders, scribes and "as many as were of the kindred of the high priest...gathered together at Jerusalem" (Acts 4:6), they asked, "By what power, or by what name, have ye done this?" (Acts 4:7b) The name was such an issue that they straightly charged him to "speak...to no man in this name" (Acts 4:17b). It appears that speaking or preaching was not the issue; it was the name of Jesus they wanted left out of the equation.

From the revelation of the name of Jesus brought by the angel Gabriel to Mary and Joseph prior to His birth to the power of the name of Jesus as demonstrated by the disciples in the Book of Acts, there is the experience of the name. It is more than mouthing pious platitudes. It is more than vain repetition of the phrase "in the name of Jesus." It is coming to grips with the tremendous release of power and experience of energy when using His name. There is power in the name of Jesus.

Peter clearly stated it was by "His name through faith in His name" that the lame man was made strong. The experience introduced them to the power of the name of Jesus. We must bring experience and relationship into revelation. There must be an exercise of faith in the name. We continue our journey by experiencing the power of the name.

The power of the name of Jesus will embolden you to do something you are called to do, that you would not do under any other circumstances. It is the power of the name of Jesus that lifts us from our own impotency to experience power in Him, bringing revival life and renewal of spirit.

Experiencing the Power of His Name

I believe the Church today is in an ongoing recovery process. Failures and frustrations experienced because of lack of power are driving God's seekers closer to classical apostolic Christianity, closer to their original mandate and power. Apostolic Christianity was not produced in a vacuum or in a hothouse of social support. It was produced in the most hostile environment possible. What came out of that environment was world-conquering, self-sacrificing faith—pure and powerful. God wants to return us to a powerful and primitive New Testament Christianity. It is a supernatural experience, defying explanation except to say, "God is at work."

An unknown writer observed, "God is sovereign, not struggling; peaceful not pouting, powerful not puny." Failure is never a divine problem; failure is a human problem that drives us to a divine solution. In that sense, even failure is redemptive.

As the miracles of the New Testament Church continued after Christ's ascension, Peter and a troupe of Christ's followers continually declared it was through His name these things were done. Many had been indoctrinated, having received shared knowledge, but had never gained experiential knowledge. They needed to experience the power of His name promised before His ascension.

As was true then, so it is true now: If the Lord can get His friends together, His enemies have had it! Yet how can God use me to write on someone else's heart if He hasn't done a number on me? They went forth from the upper room in a unity of power, wielding His name as a mighty sword against the forces of the enemy. The power of the name does not come by waving a magic wand or reciting an incantation. An experience of the name will bring you into the power of the name.

Job experienced the power of the name. He lost his family, his wealth, his health. His spiritual compass was jumping and twirling. He was left only with his experience, his revelation of the fact that the name alone could bless him. He held onto that limited exposure and proclaimed, "The Lord gave and the Lord hath taken away; blessed be the name of the Lord" (Job 1:21).

The Significance of a Name

In our world today, a person's name represents something. It calls to mind who you are, what you have accomplished, how you have lived your life. Perform a mental presidential roll call for the past couple of decades: John F. Kennedy, Lyndon Johnson, Richard Nixon, Gerald Ford, Ronald

Reagan, George Bush, Bill Clinton, George W. Bush. Each name brings to mind a face, a time in our history, and perhaps even specific incidents from their individual political careers. Their names are a summary of all they were, or are, and all they have accomplished.

In ancient Hebrew thought, an individual's name was an expression of the kind of person he was or was to become. For instance, Joseph, the son of Jacob, in naming his children, chose names with great significance to his life's story. For his firstborn, he chose Manasseh, which meant "causing to forget"—"...For God...hath made me forget all my toil, and all my father's house" (Gen. 41:51b). Then he named his second son Ephraim, which meant "double fruit"—"...For God hath caused me to be fruitful in the land of my affliction" (Gen. 41:52b).

Similarly in the Old Testament, the compound names of God each represent a specific characteristic of His manifold nature. (Later in this chapter we will take an in-depth look at each name.) His names are an extension of Himself. They are a self-revelation. God desires His name to be praised. When we praise His name, we will experience the demonstration and power of that name.

When you speak someone's name, it does not bring that person physically before you, but it may bring a mental image of that person to mind. The literal name of Jesus can be a point of contact and power with God Almighty.

His name was conceived in Heaven by the Eternal Spirit, first spoken on earth by the angels, then heard by virgin ears. What a name! It came from Heaven's mind to angel's lips through virgin spirits to world proclamation. No wonder there's power in that name!

The wise man of Proverbs said, "The name of the Lord is a strong tower: the righteous runneth into it, and is safe" (Prov. 18:10). He knew that in the experience of the name was power to still the storms of life, a safe place for God's children to find refuge and peace.

> IT CAME FROM Heaven's mind to angel's lips through virgin spirits to world proclamation.

In Acts, it is recorded, "Neither is there salvation in any other: for there is none other name under heaven given among men, whereby we must be saved" (Acts 4:12). Peter said, "Whosoever shall call on the name of the Lord shall be saved" (Acts 2:21b).

Never has a name been so powerful. "Wherefore God also hath highly exalted Him, and given Him a name which is above every name: that at the name of Jesus every knee should bow, of things in heaven, and things in earth, and things under the earth; and that every tongue should confess that Jesus Christ is Lord, to the glory of God the Father" (Phil. 2:9-11).

There is safety in His name. There is healing in His name, there is forgiveness in His name, there is hope in His name. Salvation is in His name.

Let's take a brief look at the psalmist David's perception of the name. Time and again he penned words of praise and exaltation to the name. While time and space will not permit us to list here every pertinent reference, perhaps these examples of David's thoughts about the power and effectiveness of the name of God will give us a glimpse of the experiential revelation that that David held for His name.

The name brings *joy*:

"...let them also that love Thy name be joyful in Thee" (Psalm 5:11).

"For our heart shall rejoice in Him, because we have trusted in His holy name" (Psalm 33:21).

"In Thy name shall they rejoice all the day: and in Thy righteousness shall they be exalted" (Psalm 89:16).

The name brings *praise* and *thanksgiving*:

"I will praise the name of God with a song, and will magnify Him with thanksgiving" (Psalm 69:30).

"From the rising of the sun unto the going down of the same the Lord's name is to be praised" (Psalm 113:3).

"Let them praise the name of the Lord: for His name alone is excellent; His glory is above the earth and heaven" (Psalm 148:13).

The name brings *singing*:

"So will I sing praise unto Thy name for ever, that I may daily perform my vows" (Psalm 61:8).

"Sing forth the honour of His name: make His praise glorious" (Psalm 66:2).

"Sing unto God, sing praises to His name: extol Him that rideth upon the heavens by His name JAH, and rejoice before Him" (Psalm 68:4).

The name brings *victory*:

"Through Thee will we push down our enemies: through Thy name will we tread them under that rise up against us" (Psalm 44:5).

"His name shall endure for ever: His name shall be continued as long as the sun: and men shall be blessed in Him: all nations shall call Him blessed" (Psalm 72:17).

The name brings *power* and *deliverance*:

"Because he hath set his love upon Me, therefore will I deliver him: I will set him on high, because he hath known My name" (Psalm 91:14).

"He sent redemption unto His people: He hath commanded His covenant for ever: holy and reverend is His name" (Psalm 111:9).

"Our help is in the name of the Lord, who made heaven and earth" (Psalm 124:8).

The Revelation of His Name

As we ascend the revelatory stairs to the summit of the name of Jesus by the hallowed halls of the Old Testament, we are introduced to the different dimensions of God through His multiple names. We can know God more intimately by understanding

His names, and we praise Him when meanings of His multiple names are revealed to us.

As we study and learn about the various Old Testament names of Jehovah, we must remember every revelation of His name is redemptive. Throughout the Old Testament, we learn more about Him because of His names. It is interesting to note as you study the compound Jehovah names, you will find He does not have one judgmental name. The Lamb-like nature has not yet taken on its judgmental lion-like qualities.

Above Every Other Name

His name is not a debate; it is a source of power. You can believe in divine healing, preach, and teach on it—and yet not understand the power that comes with the experience of the name. "That name" is power; "through faith in that name" is the trigger. When the disciples used His name in Acts, the lame man walked. We today have yet to release the full power of His name.

A current wave among the Body of Christ is the use of three words that are relevant to the Holy Spirit: *renewal, revival,* and *restoration.* There is a tremendous revelatory restoration of the authority of the name of Jesus cresting. Zechariah 14:9 says, "The Lord shall be king over all the earth: in that day shall there be one Lord, and His name one." To the Philippians Paul wrote, "That at the name of Jesus every knee should bow, of things in heaven, and things in earth, and things under the earth; and that every tongue should confess that Jesus Christ is Lord, to the glory of God the Father" (Phil. 2:10-11).

We have pondered it, we have discussed it, we have debated it; but have we released it to its full power? Never allow the pride of a message to take away the glory of His power. There is no debate. His name is *"above every name"* (Phil. 2:9b). His name is above Buddha, Mohammed, and Confucius. His name is above the name of every sin and sickness that can befall us. His name is above every foe that can come against us. His name is above *every* name.

All of Israel gathered on Mt. Carmel one day with 850 prophets of Baal. Two bullocks were brought for sacrifice. The prophets of Baal were given first choice. Leaping, crying, and cutting themselves through their rituals, they did all they could to summons their gods, but not one of them showed up. The Scripture says they called on the name of their gods from morning until noon "...But there was no voice, nor any that answered..." (1 Kings 18:26). They continued all day, until the time of the evening sacrifice.

Elijah then called the children of Israel together, as he repaired the altar of the Lord that had been broken down. With twelve stones signifying the twelve tribes of Israel, Elijah built up an altar "in the name of the Lord" (1 Kings 18:32). A trench was dug, water was poured, and the attention of the prophets of Baal was riveted to the activity of Elijah. When the time came, the fire fell, the water was licked up, the wood was burned, and the stones were destroyed. "And when all the people saw it, they fell on their faces: and they said, The Lord, He is the God; the Lord, He is the God" (1 Kings 18:39).

The message of the day was, *"The Lord, He is God."* That one message makes the devil tremble. It is not the message of tongues or gifts of the Spirit, but the message of the power of the name. "Thou believest that there is one God; thou doest well: the devils also believe, and tremble" (Jas. 2:19).

At another time in Israel's history, trouble came when they created another god and worshiped a calf. They forgot the power of God displayed through Moses' rod. They no longer said, "Let me show you what the power of the God of Israel can do." They forgot it had led them out of Egypt. Instead they chose to cling to the Egyptian multiple-god mentality and worshiping of idols. Notice Aaron said, "We will have a feast to the Lord" (see Ex. 32:5). He apparently ascribed to that molten calf the proper name of God. But the Lord wanted His name attached to no other image because in God's revelatory plan the Word and the name were going to become flesh, not an idol. Is this evidence that the proper and correct thing unspoken is better than for something to be spoken in the wrong context?

The power point of release in the Old Testament was often at the invocation of a revealed name of Jehovah that embodied the character of God in expanding understanding. A cursory study shows us that the tongue finds its highest employment in the glory of His name.

Space will not allow an in-depth study of the names of Jehovah, when an entire volume could possibly be dedicated to each of them. Consequently, we will explore together the basic meanings and applications of each name of God. You can then see how His name reveals His character. And, name by name, from Old Testament Jehovah to New Testament demonstration, we will experience the power of that name.

Elohim

The name *Elohim* is derived from the word *El*—signifying one who is great and mighty. It was Elohim who was "in the beginning." It is Elohim who creates. Creative acts were orchestrated from a creative name.

"Let there be light" was spoken before the creation of the sun on the fourth day (see Gen. 1). That passage could well mean, "Let Me be seen." Some say it comes from the Hebrew word *alah*, which means to declare or swear. It signifies the absence of conflict. The Great One declares it; no one contests it. His very greatness guarantees Him the absolute right to initiate covenants and to name terms. He swore by Himself and created something out of nothing. Experience Him in His creative expression. David said, "Create in me a clean heart..." (Ps. 51:10). It was a something-from-nothing experience. All God needs to make something is nothing.

Before the sun ever kissed the horizon, creation was accomplished in the light of the glory of Elohim. He did not create the sun so He could see; God can see in the dark. What was originally seen to illuminate creation was the power of God's glory. We must tap into this original light and power source.

It is accepted that Genesis was a revelation given to Moses. He was schooled in Egypt and lived in a society that worshiped a multiplicity of gods. Revelation and power came with the name of the one true God, thus Genesis begins with the simple sentence, "In the beginning God...." It was a revelation of His existence and of His power.

Elohim speaks and it is done. "Let there be..." Three simple single-syllable words were all it took to create the firmament. All the billions of stars came into existence at the sound of His voice when it declared, "Let there be lights..." (see Gen. 1:14-19).

We also can find the creative *Elohim* demonstrated in the New Testament experience of Mary and the birth of Jesus to a virgin. We find Jesus Himself giving sight to blind eyes, hearing to deaf ears, and even life in the presence of death.

El Shaddai

El means "great." *El Shaddai* is used 48 times in the Old Testament and is frequently translated "Almighty." This title literally means "strong breasted one"—the One who completely nourishes, satisfies, and supplies.

In Genesis chapter 17, El Shaddai, the God Almighty, appears to Abram. It was upon the foundation of the name *El Shaddai* that God made covenants with Abram and changed his name to Abraham. Abraham was sustained by El Shaddai—the strong breasted one—at Mt. Moriah where he took his only son (see Gen. 22). What a revelation of the keeping and sustaining power of His name in all circumstances of life.

We again see El Shaddai in Jesus as He walked among the multitudes healing their sick, delivering them from their bondages, and feeding thousands with a few loaves of bread.

Adonai

Adonai occurs approximately 330 times in 285 verses of the Old Testament and is translated "Lord." It is a derivative of the Hebrew *adown* or *adon*, meaning "controller, sovereign, lord, master, owner." It simply means He owns and rules over everything. While it is possible to know Him as Savior but not experience Him as Lord, the very fact that one of His names is *Adonai* lends credence to the concept that He wants to be Lord of everything in our lives. Understanding this dimension of His name and releasing ourselves to His lordship will change our lives. It indicates lordship on His part; stewardship and submission on ours.

Jehovah

Jehovah. This name is used over 6,800 times. It means "to be, the self-existent one." It speaks of the eternal and unchanging nature of God. This name, which literally means "I AM" is what God used to instruct Moses in Exodus chapter 3. You can understand why Jesus Christ confounded the Pharisees in John chapter 8 when He proclaimed, "Before Abraham was, I am" (Jn. 8:58)!

Jehovah was the most venerated name of God in the Old Testament. The Hebrews were fearful of verbalizing it. They often substituted it with *Adonai.* So fearful were they of pronouncing this name that they apparently removed the vowels and came up with what has been translated as Jehovah. In the Hebrew it actually looks like "YHWH." When they spoke what they considered the unutterable name, they had to wash themselves and their clothes. If they wrote it on a scroll, the same ritual cleansing was required. Some scholars have chosen Yahweh.

Accents and dialects change. Words can vary with each translation. It is impossible for us to know exactly how Moses pronounced this name. Possibly the true name was lost from pronunciation in the Old Testament so that it might be revealed in the New. The Old Testament is the New Testament concealed; the New Testament is the Old Testament revealed. So it is with the mighty God.

A noted Jewish commentator of the Middle Ages, Moses Maimonidas wrote, "All the names for God that occur in the Scriptures are derived from His works except one and that is Jehovah and this is called the plain name because it teaches plainly and unequivocally of the substance of God."

In Exodus 3:14, speaking to Moses, God instructed him to tell the children of Israel, "I AM hath sent me to you." I AM—the self-existent one—dependent on no one or nothing outside Himself. He is self-existent and self-sufficient.

There are other names connected with the name *Jehovah*. They are often referred to as the redemptive or compound names, the covenant names of God, because they show us a manner in which the covenant God deals with covenant children.

In John chapter 8, as the Jews were questioning Jesus, He said to them, "Verily, verily, I say unto you, Before Abraham was, I am" (Jn. 8:58). Old Testament Jehovah—New Testament Jesus; in Greek the word means, "Jehovah Savior."

El-Olam

El-Olam is a name of God found in Genesis 21:33, when a dispute concerning the watering of sheep could not be solved. Abimelech and Abraham built an altar and called on El-Olam, the God of mysteries and hidden things. The word itself is a reference to "the Eternal God." It points us to God's foreverness.[1] *Strong's Concordance* makes reference to this word meaning as "...the vanishing point, time out of mind, eternity." He has no end and no beginning. *El-Olam*—the eternal God.

Man's challenge is to obey God, not to understand Him. There are times when we do not understand situations and circumstances that arise, when we cannot clearly judge "the right thing" to do or say. At these junctures, we must build an altar over it and call on El-Olam to speak to us of the eternal, not temporal.

Jesus proclaimed to John the Revelator, "Fear not; I am the first and the last: I am He that liveth, and was dead; and, behold, I am alive for evermore…" (Rev. 1:17b-18). Then, in validating His statements to the church at Smyrna, He said: "These things saith the first and the last, which was dead, and is alive" (Rev. 2:8b).

Jehovah-Jireh

In Genesis 22:14, we find reference to *Jehovah-Jireh*. This is the story of Abraham and Isaac and a ram caught in the thicket.

The word *jireh* means "to see, to appear, to behold, certainly." This name has also been interpreted as "the Lord will provide." So the question is how did we get from "seeing" to "providing"? It's actually a quite simple transition. The word *provide* comes from two Latin words: *pro* means "first" or "before," and *vide* means to "see." The words together mean "to see before." Jehovah-Jireh is the God who sees everything beforehand and makes provision. He saw Abraham and Isaac climbing up the mountain and He saw the ram coming up the other side of the mountain to meet Abraham who faced the dilemma of his lifetime. So He placed the ram in the thicket and provided a sacrifice. He is Jehovah-Jireh!

At the peak, when Abraham could climb no higher and go no further, he found Jehovah-Jireh. That's not the first time he called Him that. Anyone could refer to Jehovah-Jireh when they were looking at a sacrifice. But on his way up the mountain, even while God's request remained a mystery, he said to his son's inquiry, "The Lord will provide."

There are times when you must open an empty wallet or look into bare shelves and just shout into it—Jehovah-Jireh! I haven't seen it yet, but He has already gone before.

Sometimes we judge others prematurely, not allowing enough time to see what they can make of themselves or their situation. Do you think that when Jesus called Simon "the Rock" some of the disciples might have looked around and thought, *He's certainly not that!* But Jesus knew, with time, what Peter would become. He was Jehovah-Jireh to Simon because He saw before what was to be.

> I'D RATHER HAVE A promise from God than an explanation. You can live on a promise, but not on an explanation.

In time, character is developed. Experiences mold and shape us. There is the promise, and then the experience. I'd rather have a promise from God than an explanation. You can live on a promise, but not on an explanation. Promises lead to experiences. Abraham called Him Jehovah-Jireh on the way up the mountain. He is the Lord who sees what is to be as if it is already in existence and we must trust Him.

God called Gideon a man of valor even while he was hiding in the winepress and had not done anything to warrant the honorable label. God saw in him something that needed an expression and He called it out of him. Before Saul was Spirit-filled, before he was baptized, he was simply on a roundabout journey to find Jehovah-Jireh. Before his Christ-encounter, God had already called him a chosen vessel (see Acts 9:15).

Jehovah Rapha

A crisis is at hand. The children of Israel had wandered three days in the wilderness with no water. When they arrived at Marah, they found the waters bitter. "And the people murmured against Moses, saying, What shall we drink?" (Ex. 15:24) Moses cried to the Lord for an answer to their dilemma. The reply was simple: "Listen carefully to the voice of the Lord your God. I will bring none of the diseases of the Egyptians on you. I am Jehovah Rapha, the Lord who healed you" (Ex. 15:26, author's translation). Sometimes we need help and healing for bitter situations. It is then that Jehovah Rapha steps in and says, "Healing is what I am."

Since Jesus is the same yesterday, today, and forever, only He can go into our past and touch and heal bitter experiences that haunt us. The past is a good place to learn from, but it is a bad place to live.

I have personally observed the presence of Jehovah-Rapha in the enunciation of the name of Jesus. In a tent meeting years ago in a small southern city, I was looking at a woman on the front row, not 15 feet from where I stood. She had a tumor on her forehead as big as my fist. There was a scar beneath, indicating that something had already once been removed and then recurred. The prophet of God who was speaking said, "He can send His Word and heal you!" While I watched, that huge tumor disappeared. The woman reached her hand up and touched a flat forehead. There was a shout of joy as she said, "It's gone!" I have seen cripples throw down their crutches, the weak push their wheelchairs away, and the blind open their eyes. But there will never be physical healing until you first experience the power of the name of the Healer.

Jehovah Nissi

"The Lord is my Banner!"—a name resounding with triumph. It is a proclamation that God's holy presence and promises will continually identify His people as His own.

And Moses built an altar, and called the name of it Jehovah-nissi: for he said, "Because the Lord hath sworn that the Lord will have war with Amalek from generation to generation (Exodus 17:15-16).

In this particular passage the banner is a rallying point for the troops. This is not the last fight but it is a place for us to come together and go forth triumphantly. It is a statement that from generation to generation there will be victory for God's children.

What an experience! Amalek was in the path of God's people. He was contesting their right to be there. Moses told Joshua, "Go down in the valley and take him on! I'm standing on the mountain with the rod of God" (see Ex. 17:9). There is always a relationship between the rod on the mountain and the battle in the valley. Power comes out of relationship. They experienced the victorious banner of the Lord that day!

You will never succeed until you first see yourself as a threat to the devil. Moses caught a glimpse of this. He was invoking the powerful name of Jehovah, declaring "God is our banner. He is our identity. He is our gathering pole. Stay with the standard." He saw them as victorious!

A banner was a standard or a flag. Though each of the tribes had a different flag, they were still one Israel. The unity of their concept of the God of Deuteronomy 6:4 transcended all tribal differences. They went into the fight as one unit. They broke up as families under different banners. We must either commit ourselves to the fight and victory or stay behind the lines because, as Moses declared, this is not the last battle you're going to fight (see Ex. 17:16)!

The very character of God is in the banner of victory. The gifts represent God's power; the fruit His character. Power flows out of character. You do not know people by their gifts, but by their fruit. There are those who will say, "We have cast out devils and done many mighty works and miracles..." and He will declare, "I never knew you...I don't recognize gifts as I recognize fruit" (see Mt. 7:15-23).

Not just calling on His name, but experiencing the God of the name at that dimension brings us into true knowledge. Too often we want the knowledge but not the experience that brings us to the knowledge. The only way we experience Him in His name is to undergo those situations that provide that kind of experience.

In the New Testament, Jesus Himself became our banner. He said, "And I, if I be lifted up from the earth, will draw all men unto Me" (Jn. 12:32).

Jehovah M'Kaddesh

We meet Jehovah M'Kaddesh in Leviticus 20:7: "Sanctify yourselves therefore, and be holy: for I am the Lord your God." He is the one who makes you holy. It is a term of sanctification.

We are set apart, not only from something but unto something. It is His presence and His presence alone that gives us any attribute of holiness. We are partakers of His divine nature. A life of holiness does not isolate you; it insulates you.

Hardness is not holiness. If the devil could, he'd drive holiness out of our hearts and into our fists. Whatever holiness is, we need to learn its definition because the Book of Hebrews said that without it no man can see the Lord. It is more than a doctrine; it is an experience. That's why the seraphim cried, "Holy! Holy! Holy!" The Bible speaks of holy garments, holy spirits, a holy city. His holiness is experienced externally, internally, and eternally.

Trust His holiness and experience his holiness. He is Jehovah M'Kaddesh.

In Revelation, the sound of "Holy! Holy! Holy!" previously written in Isaiah echos around the throne in eternity. "Worthy is the Lamb that was slain to receive power, and riches, and wisdom, and strength, and honour, and glory, and blessing"(see Rev. 4:8-11). Jesus Christ—the Lamb slain—Jehovah M'Kaddesh.

Jehovah-Shalom

Jehovah-Shalom is reference to "the God of peace" and is found in Judges 6:24: "Then Gideon built an altar there unto the Lord, and called it Jehovah-Shalom: unto this day it is yet in Ophrah of the Abiezrites."

The people were impoverished, suffering under judgment of the Midianites. Gideon was threshing wheat when an angel of the Lord came and sat under an oak tree. The angel, bearing the message of Jehovah-Jireh who saw what was to be, said to Gideon, "The Lord is with thee, thou mighty man of valor" (Judg. 6:12b). Gideon might not have been sure who he was, but Jehovah-Jireh knew. Gideon built an altar, brought meat and broth and put them on the rock, and presented them to the angel. The angel reached out with his staff, touched the flesh and unleavened cakes, and the sacrifice was consumed by fire.

God spoke to Gideon and said, "Peace be unto thee; fear not: thou shalt not die" (Judg. 6:23b). Gideon exclaimed aloud, "Jehovah Shalom!" God is peace.

In a time of war, when Gideon found himself in despair and depressed, he found that God not only gave peace, He was peace. The battle was not yet won, but He was peace. Gideon was traveling with a Word from the Lord and peace. In a fearful situation, God revealed Himself as the God of peace.

We see the Peace-Speaker on the Sea of Galilee. The Gospel writer tells us: "And He arose, and rebuked the wind, and said unto the sea, Peace, be still. And the wind ceased, and there was a great calm" (Mk. 4:39). Jesus spoke peace to the troubled-hearted, and many were delivered from unclean and tormenting spirits.

Jehovah Rohi

The oft quoted and well-loved passage of Psalm 23 begins, "The Lord is my shepherd...." David, the shepherd boy, introduces us to Jehovah Rohi. God is our shepherd, our caretaker and companion.

The twenty-third Psalm is a portrayal of the Shepherd's relationship with His beloved sheep. The promise is for still waters, souls restored, heads anointed, cups running over— flanked by goodness and mercy. All of this because He is our Rohi—our Shepherd. As we follow Him, sometimes we are made to lie down in green pastures. Sometimes He says to us, "Lie down long enough where you are right now and it'll green up."

In Revelation 7:17, John glimpsed Jehovah Rohi as he wrote, "For the Lamb which is in the midst of the throne shall feed them, and shall lead them unto living fountains of waters: and God shall wipe away all tears from their eyes." He will always be our Shepherd. He will still lead us even then to fountains of water. And, the caring Shepherd will wipe away all tears.

What a concept—the Lamb Himself becomes the Shepherd. There is a tremendous principle here. That man who cannot follow will never lead. The Lamb of God who followed the will of the eternal Spirit to the cross is now the predestined Lord of the universe.

Jehovah Tsidkenu

Jeremiah 23:5-6 reads, "Behold, the days come, saith the Lord, that I will raise unto David a righteous Branch, and a King shall reign and prosper, and shall execute judgment and justice in the earth. In his days Judah shall be saved, and Israel shall dwell safely: and this is his name whereby he shall be called, The Lord our Righteousness—and we find Jehovah Tsidkenu.

The only way we can be made righteous is by experiencing this dimension of His name. Paul wrote in First Corinthians 1:31,

"...Christ...is made unto us...righteousness..." He is our righteousness. I am redeemed only as I experience His righteousness.

Calvary purchased for sinners the righteousness of God in Christ. One writer said that it was there that righteousness and peace kissed each other and Jesus became righteousness personified. Calvary bought the right to be righteous.

Not only did He reveal His righteousness to Israel, but He also is the God of our righteousness! We can never in ourselves be righteous; only through Him alone can we attain righteousness. As we ponder our own human frailties and the hopeless and helpless task of establishing our own righteousness what great relief to realize that by His magnificent name—Jehovah Tsidkenu—He provides what He commands.

The word *Tsidkenu* means "to be stiff or straight." In simple terms it means "to be right." Righteousness is straight and narrow. Truth is always narrow. A pound is 16 ounces, never 15. A foot is 12 inches; $1 + 1 = 2$, not 3. God's measurements are exact. Some things we preach against may not be sin but avoiding them will keep you from sin.

If the devil attempts to intimidate you by reminding you of your past, remind him of his terrible past, remind him of his horrible present, and remind him of his eternally fiery future.

In First Corinthians 15:34a we are instructed to "Awake to righteousness, and sin not." His righteousness working in us keeps us from sin. His righteousness in us sustains us. Isaiah wrote, "...His arm brought salvation unto Him; and His righteousness, it sustained Him" (Is. 59:16). It is not by our own might or power but it is Jehovah Tsidkenu working in us.

There is a poem that reads:

I once was a stranger to grace and to God,
I knew not my danger, and felt not my load;
Though friends spake in rapture of Christ on a tree,
Jehovah Tsidkenu was nothing to me.

When free grace awoke me, by light from on high
Then legal fears shook me, I trembled to die;
No refuge, no safety, in self could I see;
Jehovah Tsidkenu my Savior must be.

My terror all vanished before the sweet name;
My guilty fears banished, with boldness I came
To drink at the fountain, life-giving and free;
Jehovah Tsidkenu is all things to me!

Author Unknown

John, in Revelation, wrote, "And I saw heaven opened, and behold a white horse; and He that sat upon him was called Faithful and True, and in righteousness He doth judge and make war" (Rev. 19:11). When all is said and done—when we have fought a good fight, finished the course, kept the faith— Jehovah Tsidkenu will return and through His righteousness put away for the final time all unrighteousness!

Jehovah Shammah

"It was round about eighteen thousand measures: and the name of the city from that day shall be, The Lord is there" (Ezek. 48:35). The presence of God means everything.

God's children were captives in Babylon, but God was there. He is not "the great I was" nor the great "I shall be"; He is the great I am. The generation to whom He spoke were captives of circumstances over which they had no control. But God was there! He is the ever-present, eternally existent One!

The city was to be named Jehovah-Shammah—the Lord is there. There's a better day coming. Captivity will not always reign. The Lord whom you seek shall suddenly come to His temple.

The glory that departed in Ezekiel's day returned to the temple when Jesus walked in at the tender age of 12 years old. It came again to the temple on the Day of Pentecost when the Holy Spirit fell on those gathered. It continually comes to us today for we are now His temple.

Moses said, "Show me Your glory." God said, "I'll show you My goodness." (See Exodus 33:18-19.) You must experience His goodness, know that He's there even in the hard places before you ever see His glory. There may not be a bumper crop every year—but He is always there. You may have a sickness in your body or in your spirit to contend with, but He is always there. You may not win every battle, but He is there in your defeats as well as in your victories.

He was there with Ezekiel in Babylon as he prophesied to Israel about a city that would be named Jehovah Shammah— the Lord is there. He was present with Miriam as she guarded a tiny ark in the Nile River. He was in the king's court with Esther. He was in the battle with Deborah. He was there with Paul in the storm saying, "Fear not!" He is present with you today, where you are, whatever your circumstances!

If your back is to the wall, He is present! If your child is sick, He is present! If your home is falling apart, He is present!

If pain is consuming your body and deteriorating your spirit, He is present! If you've lost your job and unemployment looms in your future, He is present! If your bank balance is zero and the bills are still due—He is present! If your heart is broken and your spirit wounded, He is present! He is always present!

Jehovah Shammah is the last revelatory name of God written in the Old Testament and it will be the last revelatory name we will experience when our feet touch that street of gold and we realize He is present! Jehovah Shammah was present in Babylon in captivity; He will be present in the eternal city of deliverance!

He did not deliver Daniel from being thrown into the den of lions; He was present there with him. Shadrach, Meshach, and Abednego walked through a fiery furnace experience; Jehovah Shammah was there in the fire with them. The Red Sea looked impossible to Moses and the children of Israel, but God was there to lead them through it. God was present with Joseph in the pit of abandonment. He was present with Job in his suffering. He was present with David facing a giant. He was present with Peter in the prison. God is a present God! He is present with you right now! He is Jehovah Shammah.

He is present in the present! He is present when you are alone, forsaken by friends and family. He is present when you are battling depression and feelings of despair. He is present when you are in turmoil and seeking peace. He is present when you are afraid, when you are confused, when you have failed. He is always present!

In Psalm 23:4 we hear David's cry, "...Thou art with me...." Whether it is in green pastures, by still waters, in the presence of enemies, in the valley of the shadow—it matters not. The Good Shepherd is ever near. "Thou art with me." The Lord is present. "Lo, I am with you alway, even unto the end of the world" (Mt. 28:20b). In any circumstance, He is there. He is at hand all the days of our lives, and when we reach that city built four square He will be there—no longer an unseen Presence— but we will see Him as He is!

The Forgotten Name

Now we come to what I refer to as "the forgotten name." More often than not this one is not included in the list of Jehovah names in the Old Testament. Yet it is part and parcel of who He is—a jealous God. Jealousy means to be intolerant of rivalry, and God will not tolerate a rival in our heart for His affections. He is Jehovah-Qanna (see Ex. 20:5). This is a character-describing name of God we have often overlooked. Jehovah-Qanna— the jealous God.

Jealousy can be sin. Often it is marked by such traits as resentment, envy, suspicion. So is it possible—can God be jealous?

In Deuteronomy 6:4-10, the children of Israel were instructed to bind the Word of God on their hands and heads and write it on the doorposts and gates of their homes. The message to them was clear and simple. The Word of God should control your thoughts and imaginings of your mind. It should also control what happens in your home.

Has there ever been a time when God did not demand all? He knew Israel would be blessed but would then allow their possessions to separate them from Him. He wanted them to remember Jehovah-Qanna. He is the source of it all. This name can mean "jealous" as in a marital relationship. It can mean "zeal with fury." When people get jealous, zeal often follows their fury. Couched in terms of marital relationship, Jehovah in the Old Testament was Israel's husband much as we refer to the New Testament Church as the Bride of Christ.

Isaiah said, "For thy Maker is thine husband" (Is. 54:5a). He referred to Israel as an adulterous wife who provoked His jealousy. "I shall judge you as women who commit adultery—I shall bring you the blood of wrath and jealousy."[2] God has a jealous wrath, which is to be greatly feared by those who claim to love Him.

In the Gospel of John, when Jesus went to the temple and saw them selling merchandise, He said, "...the zeal of Thine house has eaten Me up..." (Jn. 2:17). He was consumed with jealousy and had to clean house! He did not choose that moment to preach an elaborate sermon on the mount, nor did they take any time to sing songs or hymns.

According to Matthew's account, Jesus rode into the city on a donkey that day and no doubt passed many who were sick and afflicted—men, women, and children who needed His attention. Yet, He did not pause to heal even one. His mind was fixed on the house (see Mt. 21). There are times when He is present among us, and does not heal—there is no sermon, there are no songs. He is there to clean the house!

He deals with us in fiery indignation. He is a jealous God saying, "That's not supposed to go on in My house." His jealousy is for our protection. It is not competitive jealousy, but jealousy born of love and total ownership.

The Names of Who He Is

In this chapter we have looked at eight covenant or redemptive names. They have revealed His character; they have revealed our need. Experience them for a revelation of His power.

If the cupboard is bare or the wolf is at the door, call on *Jehovah-Jireh* instead of giving up! Shout it into your empty cupboard. Open it and find that He has provided!

If sickness invades, shout the name, *Jehovah Rapha*!

If you are tempted to raise the white flag of surrender, call on *Jehovah Nissi*—the Lord our banner.

Feeling abandoned? Alone? Forsaken? Remember, in your darkest trial and your deepest loneliness, He is there. His name is *Jehovah Shammah*!

Is the wind of opposition howling about you? Has turmoil targeted your spirit and left you in distress? Never forget that He is *Jehovah-Shalom*. He is your peace.

These names not only indicate what we can receive; but more importantly they disclose who He is.

There Is Another Name

Do you remember the junior high school biology lesson involving a magnifying glass, sunlight, and fire? When the prism of the glass focused the ray of the sun, the result was fire. When the names of Jehovah are focused, the result is the name of Jesus. It means Jehovah Savior. It embodies the mystery of the person of God and the marvel of His work. "In Him

Dwelleth all the fulness of the Godhead...and we are complete in Him" (Colossians 2:9-10).

In Deuteronomy 12:11 we read, "Then there shall be a place which the Lord your God shall choose to cause His name to dwell there; thither shall ye bring all that I command you; your burnt offerings, and your sacrifices, your tithes, and the heave offering of your hand, and all your choice vows which ye vow unto the Lord."

Biblical names mean something. Jesus named Simon, *Peter*—which meant "a rock." It indicated that Peter was to be a part of that great structure called the New Testament Church. He was a foundational apostle. The prophets also ascribed names to their children for particular purposes. As mentioned at the beginning of the chapter, Joseph gave his sons specific names as a result of special experiences in his life. Consequently, biblical names were not simply for identification; they carried a descriptive message and even the anticipation of what the bearer was to become. Many were prophetic.

The Lord says there will be a place, which the Lord will choose, for His name to dwell. God's name contains His character, His power, His attributes. This means that all the expressions of God will be represented in one place. Can we comprehend that there would be one place on earth where God's name would dwell and it would be the effulgence of who He really is? This ultimately came to pass in Jesus Christ.

Jesus had the creative power of Elohim. He mixed mud and spittle so that sight could be given to the one blind from birth (see Jn. 9). He was El Shaddai—the strong-breasted one—when He asked the disciples, "Will you also go away?" to which they responded, "To whom shall we go? Thou hast the words of eternal life" (see Jn. 6:67-68). He was Adonai, the Master. He was the only One who knew the answer to the question, "Good Master, what must I do to inherit eternal life?" (see Lk. 18:18) He was the God-Man—Jehovah. That's why He could say, "Before Abraham was, I am" (see Jn. 8:58). He was El Olam—the God of hidden things. In Colossians 2:3 we read, "In whom are hid all the treasures of wisdom and knowledge." He fed 5,000 men, in addition to women and children, with five loaves and two fishes (see Mk. 6:32-44). He was and is Jehovah-Jireh. To the disciples caught in a storm on the Sea of Galilee He was Jehovah Shalom when He spoke three simple words, "Peace, be still" and the wind died and the rain stopped (see Mk. 4:35-41). Time and again in the Gospels we can see Him as Jehovah Rapha as He healed the sick of all manner of infirmities. He said, "If I be lifted up..." (see Jn. 12:32)—Jehovah Nissi—the Lord my Banner. "There stood by me an angel of the Lord..."—Jehovah Shammah—the Lord is There. Paul identified him in Romans 10:4 in the role of Jehovah Tsidkenu—the Lord our Righteousness when he wrote, "Christ is the end of the law for righteousness to every one that believeth."[3]

"Neither is there salvation in any other...name..." (Acts 4:12). Jesus Christ is the Alpha and Omega. Alpha is the first letter of the Greek alphabet; Omega is the last. But He is not just the "A" and the "Z," He is the total alphabet. He is not just the beginning and the ending; He is everything in between. When you say "Jesus," you've said everything. He can do anything because Jesus is everything. Jesus is the Amen of God. When you recognize His lordship you can say, "Amen." Jesus was the final word of the Father in redemption of man. God has given Him a name that's above every name. If the doctor can name a disease without a cure, an illness without remedy—I know a name that is above it.

Jesus never did anything in His own name. Rather, in John chapter 16 He instructed the apostles, "Henceforth, do it in My name." His name brings His presence. He did not need to use His own name because He was present physically. But once He had left the earth, faith in His name would invoke His presence.

You might ask, "Why make an issue over the name?" My counter question is, "Over what dimension of the name?" Suppose someone told you that you could pray, but it wasn't necessary to pray in Jesus' name? However, we are told to pray in that name (see Jn. 16:24.) It could be alleged, "Yes, you can pray for the sick but the invocation of the name of Jesus is unnecessary." But we are commanded to lay hands on the sick in that name (see Jas. 5:14). Theologians might want to purport that using the name in a renunciation of demons is not necessary or essential. But the apostles rebuked the devil in that name (see Mk. 16:17). You might think speaking His name in baptism is not important. Yet why dilute the specific instruction of the Scripture? You should baptize in His name (see Acts 2:38; 10:44-48; 19:1-5). What about the scriptural instruction of Paul to the Colossians? "...And whatsoever ye do in word or deed, do all in the name of the Lord Jesus..." (Col. 3:17). Whatever the apostles did in Jesus' name validates its use.

The name of Jesus in every dimension can seal us into a covenant relationship with God. In the book, *Corporate Anointing*, by Kelley Varner, the author cites the story in Acts chapter 2 of the Day of Pentecost when the people inquired of

Peter and the disciples, "What must we do?" Peter boldly proclaimed, "...Repent, and be baptized every one of you in the name of Jesus Christ for the remission of sins, and ye shall receive the gift of the Holy Ghost" (Acts 2:38). He writes:

> Immersion in water into the name of the Lord Jesus Christ is the first sealing of the New Covenant whereby our sins are remitted and our hearts are circumcised. It is a public declaration that we have died to sin and have arisen to walk in newness of life married to a heavenly other. As with marriage, we have received "the name of our Husband," and two have become one. You received His name in baptism. You have put on Christ. Now walk worthy of that calling. Do not take His name in vain.[4]

The name of Jesus is a package deal. Do not sacrifice a part for the whole, or the whole for a part. We are complete in Him.

Yes, I will raise the banner over the name of Jesus. Jesus was born for us. He lived for us. He died for us. He was buried for us. He rose for us. He ascended for us. He is coming back for us. Therefore I will pray in His name, lay hands on the sick in His name, rebuke the devil in His name, baptize in His name. I lay a memorial wreath at the feet of the apostle Paul who said in Colossians, "For it pleased the Father that in Him should all fullness dwell" (Col. 1:19). We are complete in Him.

Jack Taylor is attributed with the following statement: "All that God is, He is in His names. All that He is in His names, He was in Christ. All that He is in Christ, He is in us. Blessed be His name!" There is power in the experience of His name.

Jesus is the only name hell fears. He is not an issue to be debated; He is a person to be praised. And there is power in the name!

Endnotes

1. See Richard Mayhue, *Moody*, December 1998.
2. See Ezekiel 16:38 in NIV and KJV.
3. See Acts 27:23-24.
4. Kelley Varner, *Corporate Anointing*, (Shippensburg, PA; Destiny Image Publishers, 1998), p. 106.

CHAPTER 5

THE POWER OF THE HOLY SPIRIT

God is a Spirit: and they that worship Him must worship Him in spirit and in truth (John 4:24).

But the Comforter, which is the Holy Ghost, whom the Father will send in My name, He shall teach you all things, and bring all things to your remembrance, whatsoever I have said unto you (John 14:26).

But ye shall receive power, after that the Holy Ghost is come upon you... (Acts 1:8).

God is a spirit. The **power** of the Holy Spirit is the energized, activated power of the living God. The Spirit of God has always filled the universe. It was responsible for the acts of creation. He has always been present and has been evident in every age—moving upon and energizing believers in each particular era.

The Earth Begins With the Holy Spirit

We are first introduced to the work of the Holy Spirit in the Book of Genesis. Genesis 1:2 says, "And the earth was without form, and void; and darkness was upon the face of the deep. And the Spirit of God moved upon the face of the waters." This initial passage holds the key to a moving of the Holy Spirit throughout the ages.

We understand from this passage and its use of terms like "without form" and "void" and "darkness" that "In the beginning..." there was chaos—"Without form and void." God moved in the chaos and emptiness that was the beginning. Evidently, the chaotic void and darkness—the emptiness of it all—attracted God. "The Spirit of God moved upon the face of the waters."

The psalmist wrote, "Deep calleth unto deep." Conversely shallow cries to shallow. When we are deeply hungry and in need God answers the depth of our need by the depth of His Spirit. In Genesis there was darkness "on the face of the deep"—and the Spirit of God moved upon the water. God moved not on ice, but on water. When we are pliable, sensitive, yielded to Him—when we find ourselves in darkness and "over our heads"—God will move on our behalf. He is attracted to our emptiness. He responds to our deep need. The chaos, the emptiness, the darkness of our lives can create an opportune setting for the Spirit of God to move upon us.

> HE IS ATTRACTED to our emptiness. He responds to our deep need.

The Spirit Works in the Old and the New

Just as the first recorded work of the Holy Spirit was a new creation in Genesis, so in Acts chapter 2 on the Day of Pentecost would the Holy Spirit create once again. That New Testament creation was the Church of the living God.

There are many comparisons to be made between the work of the Spirit in the Old and New Testaments. Was it not the Spirit that drew the animals into the ark? Does not the Bible state that no man can come to Jesus except he be drawn by the Spirit? Observe the movings of the Spirit upon men such as Moses, Abraham, Saul, Samson, Isaiah, and other Old Testament prophets. Do we not recognize that the holy visitation that made it possible for Daniel to write the mighty words of his book was identical to that received by John on the Isle of Patmos? Consequently, certain passages of their writings are similar, because the Holy Ghost was the real author.

The Old Testament records eight occasions when the Spirit was said to be *in* men. On 25 occasions it says that the Spirit *came upon* men. The recipients of the Holy Spirit visitation in the Old Testament were a select few who were chosen by God for certain responsibilities. But the promise of Pentecost told of a day when the clouds of God's glory would literally burst with blessing—a day when all men everywhere could personally become containers of Deity.

There is nothing as interesting as the Word of God. It is different, versatile, and fascinating. Often, it is like a continued story, a serial with each new episode more exciting than the last. Each of the Old Testament dispensations ended in judgment. Yet, there was always an undertone in the voice of God that continually reminded them that something better was ahead. As we see the transitory dispensations of Conscience, Human Government, Promise, and Law, there seems to be a subplot in the Divine Author's mind. Our hearts cry out with Israel, "Oh, God where is that perpetual covenant? When will the experience come that will continue to the end of the age?"

MORE POWER TO YOU

Christ and His Church are superior in every way to all dispensational predecessors. Mercy and truth came at last in the person of Jesus Christ. It was written, "of His kingdom there shall be no end" (Lk. 1:33b). The coming of Christ in spirit form on Pentecost was the beginning of this spiritual Kingdom that would have no end. It continues to this day.

The Book of Hebrews was written to establish the superior claims of Christ above the Law. The writer tells us that Christ is fifteen ways better than the prophet. In thirty-five points He is superior to angels. In seven areas, He excelled Moses, and in five ways He is above Joshua. The writer further teaches that He is in ten ways superior to the priest, and in eight ways above Melchizedek. In seven avenues He exceeds Abraham, and His priesthood bests Aaron's in twenty-two points. His blood sacrifice touches twenty areas not included in the Old Testament system of sacrifice. He further speaks of better things in a better country. Jesus Christ is the same yesterday, today, and forever (see Heb. 13:8).

In declaring these things, it is not my reputation at stake, but God's integrity. How often have we seen an unctionless ministry swing ax handles without heads against the trees of worldliness and lukewarmness to no avail? They have lost their keen spiritual cutting edge because they refuse to admit that the Holy Spirit in all its power continues. The Holy Spirit came with attendant signs and miracles in Acts chapters 2, 8, 10, and 19. So it continues to operate in the world today.

"And it shall come to pass afterward, that I will pour out My spirit upon all flesh..." (Joel 2:28). F.B. Meyer observes that the "pour out" of Joel 2:28 could better be translated "empty out." It was as if there was a to be a cloudburst of heavenly rain. It was as though God had, in ages past, erected a heavenly reservoir, and for ages untold promises and prophecies had been poured into this reservoir and stored for a future day. Finally, the promises of God, the prophecies of the Old Testament, and the pre-figuring of Pentecost were more than the heavenly dam could contain. Suddenly, there was a rupture, and the reservoir was broken, causing the contents to rush out in one mighty stream to the lowlands of human need and environment.

Read Hosea's account of a day when there would be a former rain and then another day when there would come a latter rain (see Hos. 6:3). Rejoice at the prayers of Israel in Jeremiah chapter 50 as they beg God for a perpetual covenant. Stand with Malachi on the pinnacle of revelation as he sees the Sun of righteousness appear with healing in His wings. These humble men all thanked God for their experience, yet with anxious anticipation they looked ahead to a better day.

The Old Testament is filled with types, shadows, prefigurings, and symbols of things to come in the New Testament. I fully realize that it is impossible to build a doctrine upon a type or a symbol. However, it is perfectly scriptural to use a type or a symbol to support an already existing Bible doctrine.

The greatest work of the Holy Spirit today on earth is done through the Body of Christ, the Church. In this dimension it began on the Day of Pentecost two thousand years ago. But the door of Acts 2 actually opened on the hinges of Joel 2.

Ezekiel had a vision of water flowing from a threshold. First it was ankle deep. Then it was knee deep—waist deep— and finally "water to swim in." One symbolic interpretation of this vision can be seen in the Book of Acts. The proverbial door swung open on the Day of Pentecost. The man at the Gate Beautiful found healing in the ankle-deep waters flowing in His name. In Acts 4 the newly birthed Church is on its knees—knee deep in the water of the Spirit. Acts 5 finds the followers at the waist-deep level—where the reproductive organs of the body are—and the newly birthed church is multiplying. Finally, the count is lost—the multitudes are added, the miracles continue, and it's "waters to swim in." Ezekiel's final vision was of waters he "could not pass over." The Pentecostal experience should be something we cannot get over.

The Acts of the Holy Spirit

There are many who go window shopping through the Book of Acts. They pause in Acts chapters 1 and 2, beholding the actions of the apostles, along with Mary, the mother of Jesus, and the other disciples. With noses pressed against the window, they sigh, "Oh, if I could but have that fire, that fervor, that force." Thrill with me as the story of a continuing Pentecost unfolds through the Book of Acts. It is called the Acts of the Apostles. It would be better named the Acts of the Holy Spirit.

Pentecost produced an unparalleled spirit of unity and togetherness in the infant Church. We find such phrases as, "one accord" (Acts 2:1); "But Peter, standing up with the eleven" (Acts 2:14a); "They...did eat their meat with gladness and singleness of heart" (Acts 2:46); "They went to their own company" (Acts 4:23a); "They lifted up their voice to God with one accord..." (Acts 4:24b). There was nothing to fuse that early Church together like the fiery torch of the Holy Spirit.

It was in this spirit that Peter and John went to the temple in Acts chapter 3. The blessed man heard the words, "Silver and gold have I none; but such as I have give I thee: In the name of Jesus Christ of Nazareth rise up and walk" (Acts 3:6). It was then that the lame leaped like a hart. Luke, the physician, the author of Acts, retained some of his old pharmaceutical phrases. Eight times in chapters 2, 3, 4, and 5 he uses the word "filled." "They were filled with the Holy Ghost"; "filled with wonder and amazement"; "Then Peter, filled with the Holy Ghost." Dr. Luke knew the Great Physician, Jesus, could fill any prescription. One could observe that in meeting these people the devil must have felt like a lion in a den full of Daniels.

Which Kind of Power?

People call for power. They want it! They thrive on it! Some live for it! Some die for it! Some see power as a force that can set them free while others see it in different ways.

Byron Kaus in *Enrichment Journal* made this statement:

What about the power Pentecostals have long claimed as their own by virtue of their birthright in the Holy Spirit baptism? Unfortunately, many Pentecostal preachers today have been side-tracked by a worldly power—a power that we forget has been defeated. When we preach faithfully and get no reaction, when we counsel lovingly and couples still divorce, when the pastor down the street preaches poorly and still saves souls—we wonder where the power is. Instead of believing God's future promises, we want what we think is the sure thing and we want it now.

Also, we get caught up in the world's definition of success that bigger is better and position is power. Yet, God replaces man's versions of power with His unlikely versions, humiliating man's vision of strength by creating the cross as the symbol of strength and triumph. Our goal is to extricate ourselves from the influence of worldly power and restore ministries proper motivation. Thus, we must recognize Christ as our Savior, baptizer, healer, soon coming King who loves us, conforms us to Himself, restores our health and relationships, and will one day reign in Kingdom and power forever. It goes without saying that we must repent when the Lord convicts us of settling for alternative forms of power. For without this repentance, there can be no personal or corporate renewal.[1]

Peter Wagner, as an outside observer said, "Pentecostals have sacrificed the five big P's—power, prayer, preaching, praise, and helping the poor for one little R—respect."[2]

Faith to Receive the Power

There is no discussion that requires as much mental discipline as the subject of "How to receive the baptism of the Holy Spirit." Cooperative faith on the part of all involved is a gospel imperative if an outpouring of the Spirit is to be forthcoming. The pooling of faith was the determining factor in every New Testament outpouring. Whether it was the 120, as on the Day of Pentecost, or just two, with Philip and the Ethiopian eunuch in the Gaza desert, a unified effort saw the task accomplished.

Let the reader who has yet to receive the Spirit-filled blessing unite in faith with the author as we progress through this particular area of study and seeking. If you are in need of the baptism of the Holy Spirit, may the light of God's Word so illuminate this truth to you, that there will come an explosion of faith in you heart, and you, too, will receive it.

Paul declared, "So then faith cometh by hearing, and hearing by the word of God" (Rom. 10:17). Only as we focus our faith on God's Word can we expect it to be fulfilled. Faith must always have a focus. Our primary obligation is not to recite truths about religion, but to proclaim the saving Word.

The emphasis of the ministry of John the Baptist, forerunner of Jesus, was on the mighty Holy Spirit that was to come. Every gospel writer reiterates John's prophecy of the coming Comforter.

> *He shall baptize you with the Holy Ghost, and with fire* (Matthew 3:11b).

> *He shall baptize you with the Holy Ghost* (Mark 1:8).

> *One mightier than I cometh, the latchet of whose shoes I am not worthy to unloose: He shall baptize you with the Holy Ghost and with fire* (Luke 3:16b).

> *Upon whom thou shalt see the Spirit descending, and remaining on Him, the same is He which baptizeth with the Holy Ghost* (John 1:33b).

Note the emphasis in all four of these accounts—on the Giver, not the receiver. May we commit our thinking to exalt the mighty Baptizer, the Lord Jesus Christ Himself, as we consider the subject at hand. Why did the wisdom of the Holy Spirit dictate that every Gospel writer would mention the coming of the Spirit? Could it not be that it is because the law of human behavior says that whatever the human mind is taught repeatedly and does not reject, it will eventually believe; and what we believe, we will do? Lift us up with believing hearts!

The first step to receiving is believing. In Isaiah 11:2, the prophet Isaiah gives seven (five intellectual and two emotional) attributes of the spirit of God:

> *And the spirit of the Lord shall rest upon Him, the spirit of wisdom and understanding, the spirit of counsel and might, the spirit of knowledge and of the fear of the Lord.*

We must mentally assent to the fact that the Holy Spirit is for us today. The assertion that the Spirit was only for a select few of an earlier church era must be completely washed from our minds. We still live today in the dispensation of the Holy Spirit. To those who knock, the door will still open. Those who seek will still find. The Baptizer of Pentecost still lives. When the Church returns to Pentecost, Pentecost will return to the Church. "The fire shall ever be burning upon the altar; it shall never go out" (Lev. 6:13).

Christ Himself gave us the believing key in John 7:37-39. Notice carefully the words, "any man thirst...come...drink... believeth...receive." It does not take a theologian to comprehend that if any man is thirsty and will come to the Savior in faith believing, he will receive. This is also the promise of Acts 2:39: "For the promise is unto you...." Some approach the reception of the Spirit with their faith in reverse. They are convinced that He will only come after much seeking. This is an attitude of doubt. It is possible that we Spirit-filled preachers are partly to blame. We may have encouraged the illusion that the Holy Spirit is the most difficult thing in the world to get, and the easiest in the world to lose.

Faith is necessary to receive anything from God. "But let him ask in faith, nothing wavering. For he that wavereth is like a wave of the sea driven with the wind and tossed. For let not that man think that he shall receive any thing of the Lord. A double-minded man is unstable in all his ways" (Jas. 1:6-8). The necessity of believing without wavering is apparent from this text. Some people are double-minded and vacillate between their faith, their fears, their desires, and their doubts.

One minute they believe the promise is for them, but the very next minute they are like the tide, and recede back into the ocean of doubt. Faith is the current coin of God's Kingdom. With faith you can buy anything God has. Without it, you can buy nothing. "Now faith is the assurance (the confirmation, the title deed) of the things [we] hope for" (Heb. 11:1, AMP). When believing faith is in your heart, you have the title-deed in your hand. Every fiber of the total man must cry out in believing faith for the blessed Comforter.

The Psalmist declared, "As the hart panteth after the water brooks, so panteth my soul after thee, O God" (Ps. 42:1). Some have asserted it is dangerous for one to focus his mental facilities on seeking Holy Spirit unction. They have further cried that one could lose his mind and be driven insane. I might ask of the doubters if any mathematician ever solved a calculus problem with a divided mind. Every mental faculty of the mathematician must be poured into one channel—solving this problem. Never doubt in the dark what God spoke to you in the light.

Repent to Receive the Power

The next divine imperative is repentance. The first ministry word of John the Baptist was, "Repent" (see Mt. 3:2). The first ministry word of Jesus was, "Repent" (see Mt. 4:17). The first ministry word of Peter on the Day of Pentecost was, "Repent" (see Acts 2:38). To simply believe that you can receive the Holy Spirit is not enough. It is futile to seek to be filled without first repenting of all known sin. The eighth chapter of the Book of Acts makes it plain that a man can go through the motions of coming to Christ, and even be baptized without having fully repented. Simon the sorcerer believed and was baptized, yet it was evident from the words of Peter that his heart was not right with God (see Acts 8:9-24). The word *repent* means simply "to quit sinning." Not just to be sorry for your sins, but to be sorry enough to stop doing them is true repentance.

Jealousy, envy, and malice must be rooted from the heart by the Word of God. Filthy habits must be laid aside. Suffice it to say that we must adhere to the words of the apostle Paul who said, "Let us cleanse ourselves from all filthiness of the flesh and spirit..." (2 Cor. 7:1b).

There are those who think they are too vile and sinful to ever be received in an act of repentance. To you, the Savior says, "Him that cometh to Me I will in no wise cast out" (Jn. 6:37b). To say you are not good enough to receive the Holy Spirit is like saying you are too sick to go to a doctor. My Lord will not alter the robe of righteousness to fit the man, but when observing an act of repentance, He alters the man to fit the robe.

Let the Word of God wound your conscience deeply and indicate to you what must flee from your soul before the Comforter will come. The Holy Spirit performs two works in a man: He empties the soul of self, and then He fills the soul which He has emptied with Himself.

Following total repentance, Peter instructed us to be baptized (Acts 2:38). The eternal Spirit descended upon Jesus like a dove. Interestingly, a dove will not come to rest upon its nest if it suspects that even one twig has been moved during its absence. Instead, it will hover above the nest until it is sure that it is safe to land. I have often seen the Spirit of God hovering over those tarrying for the Holy Spirit. I have heard their stammering lips, yet the Spirit never rested upon them because there was a twig out of place. Something had not been laid upon an altar of repentance.

Mr. Moody, I must take my hat off to you for saying, "We would not have to wait long for this endowment of the Spirit if we did not have to come to the end of ourselves."[3] This is often a long road. If God were to endue us with power while we're yet filled with conceit, we would become as vain as peacocks. How blessed to know when you come to the end of your road you have just driven up in God's front yard!

Pray and Worship to Receive the Power

The Holy Spirit comes by faith, repentance, prayer, and worship:

These all continued with one accord in prayer and supplication (Acts 1:14a).

And they worshiped Him, and returned to Jerusalem with great joy; and were continually in the temple, praising and blessing God (Luke 24:52-53).

Supplication is that humble prayer growing out of a desperate need. It is the prayer of one whose only hope depends on an answer. They prayed, they supplicated, and they worshiped. It was the type of prayer uttered by David while in the wilderness of Judah, "O God, Thou art my God; early will I seek Thee: my soul thirsteth for Thee, my flesh longeth for Thee in a dry and thirsty land, where no water is; to see Thy power and Thy glory, so as I have seen Thee in the sanctuary" (Ps. 63:1-2).

Oh, Lord, do it again, do it again! Pour out of Thy Spirit upon us. Our Lord promised that those who hunger and thirst after righteousness would be filled. God-hungry men find God. God-thirsty men search until they find the river of life.

They worshiped Him. They exalted the Lamb of God, and consequently the Dove of the Spirit descended. Whenever the general presence of God settles over a congregation, reach up and claim a personal presence for yourself. Unity of mind and spirit was a hallmark of the first seekers after the Holy Spirit. So must it be today. Focus your mind upon exalting the mighty Baptizer. Do not make the mistake of seeking tongues. Tongues will come automatically, issuing spontaneously from your freshly-fired heart, when the blessed Comforter appears.

Let me hasten to add, don't reject the gifts of the Spirit either. If you keep rejecting the message of the Holy Spirit of tongues and gifts, you might eventually win the battle that you'll someday wish you had lost. Of the three manifestations of the baptism of the Holy Spirit in Acts chapter 2—fire, wind, and tongues—many individuals participated in the speaking with tongues.

Some people inquire, "Do you have to speak with tongues?" My reply is, "It's in the Book!" What do you mean, "have to"? You *get* to! It is a privilege that unites, not a partition of division. As the New Testament Church was "born again" with the outpouring on the Day of Pentecost, it was a mighty river beginning to flow:

> *And there appeared unto them cloven tongues like as of fire, and it sat upon each of them. And they were all filled with the Holy Ghost, and began to speak with other tongues, as the Spirit gave them utterance* (Acts 2:3-4).

> *For they heard them speak with tongues, and magnify God"* (Acts 10:46a).

> *And when Paul had laid his hands upon them, the Holy Ghost came on them; and they spake with tongues, and prophesied* (Acts 19:6).

Tarry to Receive the Power

The Holy Spirit comes by tarrying. I do not wish to imply that it is necessary to tarry for any given length of time in order to receive it. However, apparently, it takes some individuals longer to "die" than others. "Tarry ye in the city of Jerusalem, until ye be endued with power from on high" (Lk. 24:49b). The word *tarry* as used here means to sit down for a purpose, not to remain for a time. Tarry by the promise of God for the purpose of God until He meets you there. He always returns by way of His promise. Remove from your mind the misconception that you must tarry for a specific length of time. Tarry for the promise, and it will come to you.

The Promise of the Holy Spirit

Earlier in this chapter, we noted that the Holy Spirit is received in an act of faith. God granted to us the faith that turns the promises into fulfilled prophecies; faith that is an echo of the voice of God; faith that is the blessed antiseptic of the soul. According to the Word of God, you know that you have access. Now vitally, you are moving in to claim what is legally yours. "And whosoever will, let him take the water of life freely" (Rev. 22:17b).

Take the gift that is extended from the hand of the Savior. Faith makes the up look good, the out look bright, the in look favorable, and the future glorious. Just as you received pardon from the hand of the dying Savior, receive the Spirit from the hand of the risen Lord. The Holy Spirit is a gift. You do not have to strain after the Spirit of God. Don't simply begin to pray; expect to receive. The Holy Spirit is restful. "For with stammering lips and another tongue will He speak to this people...This is the rest..." (Is. 28:11-12).

I remember well the night I moved in, requested reservation in the Book of Acts, and God confirmed my reservation with signs following. It was a vital act of faith for me. The Holy Spirit fell upon me, and I was filled with His presence. The highest holiday of my soul was the day of the pentecostal blessing.

When an individual is baptized with water, he presents himself to the minister as a candidate. He does not have to do anything except yield to the one who is to immerse him. Something is done to him. Likewise, when a person desires to be baptized with the Holy Spirit, he needs only to present himself as a candidate, and Jesus baptizes him with the Holy Spirit.

There are two types of promises. One is based on the sovereign will of God. It will be fulfilled regardless of what happens. The Messiah was promised, and He came. Likewise, the second coming is inevitable; He promised and He will return again.

There are other promises, however, that even though they are spoken by God, will not come to pass without prayer and preparation. These must be prayed into fulfillment by the servants of God. So often we lack faith in God's promises, and seem to think that if the wall of Jericho is going to fall the seventh day, there ought to be a crack in it by the sixth. The promise of the Holy Spirit will never come to pass until you pray and believe it into fulfillment. The promise of rain was given to the prophet Elijah in First Kings 18:1, but he did not sit in the shade and wait until God was ready. He went up on the mountain and prayed it into fulfillment. God is now ready to fill your hungry soul with the Holy Spirit. Claim it in an act of faith. The promise is unto you!

Endnotes

1. Byron Kaus, The General Council of the Assemblies of God, 2002.

2. C. Peter Wagner.

3. D.L. Moody.

CHAPTER 6

THE POWER OF A WHISPER

And he arose, and did eat and drink, and went in the strength of that meat forty days and forty nights unto Horeb the mount of God. And he came thither unto a cave, and lodged there; and, behold, the word of the Lord came to him, and he said unto him, What doest thou here, Elijah? And he said, I have been very jealous for the Lord God of hosts: for the children of Israel have forsaken Thy covenant, thrown down Thine altars, and slain Thy prophets with the sword; and I, even I only, am left; and they seek my life, to take it away. And He said, Go forth, and stand upon the mount before the Lord. And, behold, the Lord passed by, and a great and strong wind rent the mountains, and brake in pieces the rocks before the Lord; but the Lord was not in the wind: and after the wind an earthquake; but the Lord was not in the earthquake: and after the earthquake a fire; but the Lord was not in the fire: and after the fire a still small voice. And it was so, when Elijah heard it, that he wrapped his face in

*his mantle, and went out, and stood in the entering
in of the cave. And, behold, there came a voice unto
him, and said, What doest thou here, Elijah? And
he said, I have been very jealous for the Lord God
of hosts: because the children of Israel have forsak-
en Thy covenant, thrown down Thine altars, and
slain Thy prophets with the sword; and I, even I
only, am left; and they seek my life, to take it away.
And the Lord said unto him, Go, return on thy way
to the wilderness of Damascus: and when thou
comest, anoint Hazael to be king over Syria: and
Jehu the son of Nimshi shalt thou anoint to be king
over Israel: and Elisha the son of Shaphat of
Abelmeholah shalt thou anoint to be prophet in thy
room* (1 Kings 19:8-16).

"And after the fire, a still small voice."

In this audio sensitive world, let's explore the unique
power of a whisper. God seldom yells at His children. More
often than not He comes to us in what one translation calls, "a
gentle whisper" (1 Kings 19:12 NIV). His can be the simple,
"still small voice."

A Prophet Running Scared

His name was Elijah. He was a mighty prophet of the God
of Israel. He was the restorer of the Law. Leonard Ravenhill
said, "When Elijah prayed, fire fell. When Elijah prayed, rain
fell. When Elijah prayed, prophets fell. He altered the course of
nature and strangled the economy of a nation, because he had

an uncanny hold on God."[1] He knew how to pray. He was a mighty prophet and a hero for the ages.

After having experienced one of his greatest victories, Elijah received a letter from Mrs. Ahab, better known as Jezebel. The message was short and to the point: "As the rest of the prophets are (which being interpreted meant *dead*) so shall you be by this time tomorrow" (see 1 Kings 19:2).

His decision was less than heroic. He panicked. He ran.

I do not personally believe Jezebel really wanted to kill Elijah. If she had, she would have sent an executioner, not a threatening message. What she wanted is what she got—for Israel to see their "hero" running scared. If she had killed him, he would have become a martyr and been remembered forever as a hero. But by frightening him into running away, Israel would see him as a coward and that was the precise result she hoped to achieve.

Jezebel's threats finally put the prophet on the run. He had already been under a tremendous amount of pressure. She hung wanted posters hung in every post office in Israel: "Wanted Dead or Alive: Elijah. Call Jezebel collect." So far, he had eluded her. This time, however, she had gotten too close. He was weary and he was scared. The prophet of God found himself running on empty in the fast lane.

Study the Scripture and you'll read how he was fed by an angel twice. Then, on the strength and sustenance of that angel food, he made the 40-day journey to Horeb. It was there he caved in. Oftentimes pressure will do that to you. You can run just so long. You can carry your load alone for just so long.

Then you cave in. Elijah went into a dark cave, avoiding the light, and held himself a solitary pity party.

But out of the darkness, God spoke to him and said, "What are you doing here?" God wasn't talking about the cave. He wasn't talking about Horeb. He was talking about Elijah's spiritual position. "Why are you in this condition, Elijah?" God said, "Come out here and stand." So Elijah obeyed the voice of God and went and stood as the Lord had commanded him to do.

Not in Earth, Wind, or Fire...

As Elijah was standing upon the mountain, first, there came a mighty wind. It shook the mountain; rocks began to tumble down the inclines. But according to the Scripture, God was not in the wind. Next there came an earthquake. The whole mountain shook. But again, according to the Scripture, God was not in the earthquake. Then came a fire. But God wasn't there either.

Just because God did not appear to Elijah in these forces of nature at Horeb doesn't mean that God is never in wind, or never shows Himself in an earthquake, or never makes Himself known in fire. Those on the Day of Pentecost witnessed Him display Himself in wind. The three Hebrew children knew Him as He manifest Himself in their fire. The Philippian jailer could testify to the power of His earthquake. On the other hand, even though fire fell on Job's sheep and his servants called it "the fire of God," we know it wasn't. All fire that allegedly falls on the sheep is not the fire of God. So the message to Elijah was that God is not in every wind, nor every fire, nor every earthquake.

Can you imagine Elijah, standing there at the mouth of the mountainside cave? What an astounding display of power! What a frightening experience to find yourself in a hurricane-strength wind—trying to keep your balance while the earth shakes beneath you—mopping sweat from your brow as the fire passes by. Elijah retreated to the cave again. But God called him back out and this time spoke to him—not in wind, earthquake, or fire—but in a still, small voice. Elijah was about to learn the power of a whisper. He was hearing the gentle whisper of God.

The face of the prophet was symbolic of his calling and vocation. When Elijah wrapped his face in his mantle, he was trying to hide his calling. He was covering his ears from what he was hearing. Strange isn't it—that he didn't cover himself in any of the other circumstances. It was that still small voice that elicited that response.

...But in the Whisper

Too often we seek the spectacular from God. "Oh, God, if I could just see some dynamic manifestation! Just shake this place! Let your fire fall and let me witness it. Let a spiritual tornado come through here and pick me up and deposit me in just the exact location you would have me be." However, He wants us to hear His voice—still and small.

Because a whisper prevailed over wind, fire, and earthquake, today we can know that a word from the Lord is more powerful than any force of nature. From the whisper, Elijah got direction for the rest of his ministry. The voice of God, even in a whisper, is more powerful than any other manifestation of that voice.

We look for the super-kinetic. I fear we have accepted the spectacular as a substitute for the supernatural. We seek the big show. While there is nothing wrong with wind, and fire, and earthshaking, it may be that God wants you to be still enough for long enough to be drawn from your cave of self-pity and self-serving to hear His gentle whisper. Just as the Lord said to Elijah, "Okay. Go anoint Jehu. Go anoint Hazael. Anoint Elisha to take your place," His whisper to you will be so powerful that you can exit the cave, never again doubting that you have heard His voice and know His direction for the rest of your life. You must have a grasp of a true victory from God,

> I FEAR WE HAVE accepted the spectacular as a substitute for the supernatural.

and a clear glimpse of His direction for your life, to anoint someone else to take your job.

The men God instructed Elijah to anoint represented three generations. One whisper was powerful enough for all three. It wasn't because Elijah had seen some manifestation. It was because he had heard the voice of the Lord. When you have a word from the Lord, you have something more powerful than any manifestation that comes as a result of a visit from God.

God can visit the place where you sit now reading this book. He can shake you, literally. You can leave where you are and say, "God shook me." But the important question is, "What did God say to you?" "I don't know what He said but I won't ever forget that He shook the place where I was." That's good, but the question is still: "What did God say to you?"

It is the gentle whisper of God—when He comes down and speaks specifically to you—that will change your life. The wind, fire, and earthquake preceded the word of the Lord. But God was not in those things. God was in the whisper.

God is not in every wind. God is not in every fire. God is not in every earthquake. "Man shall not live by bread alone, but by every word that proceedeth..." (Mt. 4:4b). You can get one word from God and it is more powerful than wind, or fire, or earthquake.

God called this man out of the cave and said, "Stand right here." It doesn't tell us how long Elijah stood there to see the wind, the fire, and the earthquake. But sometimes God makes us stand still and notice the things that He is not in before He will speak to us. Haven't you had situations in your life that made you say, "God is not in that"? And in the aftermath, if you listened closely, you could hear the still small voice of God in your life.

There is a need in our lives for the powerful whisper of God. How different our lives will be when we hear it, when we can leave a place of prayer with a personal word from the Lord. There have been times when I have had to stand and see things I knew God was not in. I never knew why I had to observe them except that God ordained it, much like Elijah was never given an explanation. If you can't get a fresh word from the Lord, you go on the last word He gave you. Sometimes the first word you get is to come out of your cave and stand still. Before you can ever be commissioned to go forward in your walk with God, He may have some things He wants you to see.

A Whisper of Sacrifice

Sometimes we are required to yield to circumstances for which we are not responsible. Isaac was bound to an altar because of a covenant his father had made. You've never lived until you've been bound to an altar by circumstances not of your own making. Yes, on occasion we must yield to circumstances beyond our control. Oftentimes, though, we resist the very circumstances God has sent to develop us. Faith is not *believing* God in spite of circumstances; faith is *obeying* God in spite of consequences.

Isaac did not have a lot of answers, but he yielded to the circumstances. He did it on the basis of one whisper. "Come up the mountain." Abraham said, "The Lord will provide" (see Gen. 22:8). *Jehovah-Jireh.* That's all he heard. *Jehovah-Jireh.* Where's the sacrifice? *Jehovah-Jireh.* Lay down on the altar? *Jehovah-Jireh.* "Let Me tie you up." *Jehovah-Jireh.* "Let Me prepare the fire. *Jehovah-Jireh.* All he had was a whisper...but it was a powerful word.

None of it made any sense. But the promise still stood. God said He would provide. Abraham drew the knife back. *Jehovah-Jireh.* Isaac had a word from the Lord and it was more powerful than the fire his father had, than the wind of circumstances blowing on Mt. Moriah. He knew that he had a word from the Lord. He couldn't explain it. That word was, "Stay on the altar." All of us have experienced things we can't explain.

Sometimes, you have to go a long time on the last word God gave you.

A Whisper Can Last a Long Time

Personally I've had similar experiences. No, not on a mountaintop with fire and physical sacrifice. But I've had circumstances in my life that required that I go a long time between words from the Lord. I became confused, perhaps even a little disoriented as events transpired around me and I was still clinging to my last word from the Lord. As Elijah did, I've had to go the proverbial "40-day journey" on the last word I received. I've had to remind myself, "I have this word from the Lord and it hasn't changed nor been replaced with a fresher word. This is all I have—and all I have to go on."

God spoke to Noah one time and told him to build an ark. As far as we can tell, Noah didn't hear from God again for at least one hundred years. Now, if it had been me and God had told me to build a way out for my generation, after about the first 25 years I would have wanted to know, "Lord, are You sure this is what You want me to do? Come tell me again." And I feel certain that by the 50-year mark a little verbal reassurance would have been welcomed.

Can you imagine the questions in his own mind? Much less the questions from his family and friends? Can't you just imagine Mrs. Noah—Rain? What is rain? And when are you going to get that thing out of my front yard? Noah, honey, are you sure you heard right? Maybe you were a little confused..."

But Noah had a word from the Lord and he didn't need anything else. The power of that whisper was enough to build an ark for that generation's safety. He built a way out for his generation.

No doubt there was a hurricane of irreverent words swirling around them. But Noah was listening for that certain voice and that certain sound that is more powerful than the wind, more potent that the earthquake, more puissant than the fire.

The Whisper of the Word

The first ministerial utterance of Jesus after His public anointing is found in Matthew 4:4: "It is written...." Satan's first recorded utterance, found in the Book of Genesis was a question: "Hath God said...?" (see Gen. 3:1) Satan is always about the business of raising doubts and asking questions. Jesus, on the other hand, turns question marks into exclamation points. He is always raising faith to its apex. "It is written."

Sometimes voices will call out to you, "Hath God said? Did you really hear from Him? Do you truly have a word from the Lord?" It is in those hours that you must come around and pick up the Spirit of Jesus Christ and say, "It is written. I have a word from the Lord and I am going to proceed on the power of that word." Even if the word was nothing more than a whisper, that whisper is powerful enough to obey unequivocally.

If we don't trust the arm of the flesh when it is engaged for us, why should we believe or fear the arm of the flesh when it is engaged against us. You may say, "I want to dance before the Lord for an hour. I wish I could see fire fall in this place." That would be good. But better yet, if you can get one whisper that you know is from God, it will be enough to last for three generations. You might be able to imprint something on the next generation based on something you heard.

Let's take a look at Second Peter 1:16-20:

For we have not followed cunningly devised fables, when we made known unto you the power and coming of our Lord Jesus Christ, but were eyewitnesses of His majesty. For He received from God the Father honour and glory, when there came such a voice to Him from the excellent glory, This is My beloved Son, in whom I am well pleased. And this voice which came from heaven we heard, when we were with Him in the holy mount. We have also a more sure word of prophecy; whereunto ye do well that ye take heed, as unto a light that shineth in a dark place, until the day dawn, and the day star arise in your hearts: knowing this first, that no prophecy of the scripture is of any private interpretation.

"We saw Him transfigured. We saw the glory coming forth from Him. We heard His words." Peter continued to say though, "I have something better than this for you...a more sure word of prophecy." He tells you what that sure word is—the Scripture. It is the Word of God. Peter saw Him transfigured. He was on the mountain. He saw the vision. He heard the voices. Yet he said, "I've got something better than that." The Scripture.

We say, "If I could have only been there! I wish I could have seen Him transfigured!" But you and I have something better than that. You know why? If you saw visions, were visited by angels, heard voices, witnessed fire falling, felt His wind, remembered the place where you sit had been shaken five years before when life brought pressure to bear on you, you might wonder, "What was that?" "Did it really happen?" "Does it matter now?"

But when you have the Word you can claim every day, every week, every month, you have the Word from the Lord that is timeless. I thank God for visions and dreams. I thank God for angelic visitations. But I have the Word and it is more powerful than any other manifestation. I have found a more sure way! Thank God for the Bible!

It may be that you are reading through the Word of the Lord and a Scripture whispers to you and says, "This promise is yours." You can go back next week and it will still be there. You can go back five years from now and it will still stand. And at the very end of your life it will still be there, still standing true, and still be yours.

That is the power of the Word...that is the power of a whisper!

Please do not misunderstand me. I am not in any way discounting miracles. But miracles are in the seeds...and the seed is the Word of the Lord. If you get the seed, you'll get the miracle. "Thy word have I hid in mine heart..." (Ps. 119:11). If you get the seed of the Word, it will root out doubt. It will cast down fear. It will calm the anxious heart. All it has to be is a whisper.

Obeying the Whisper

Obedience releases revelation; disobedience withholds it. When you are willing to simply be obedient to what you are told, the Word can last a lifetime. He will never tell you something privately that contradicts the written Word. Be obedient and it will speak life to you!

First Samuel 15:23a reads, "For rebellion is as the sin of witchcraft, and stubbornness is as iniquity and idolatry." Do you know what the difference is between rebellion and stubbornness? A rebellious man says, "I won't do it." A stubborn man says, "I'll do it, but I'll do it my way." Stubbornness is as idolatry. Do you know why? Because a stubborn man worships his own opinion.

You would think it quite ludicrous if you entered your church Sunday morning, and found the communion table had been replaced by a statue of Buddha, and the early arrivals were gathered at the front chanting, "Buddha! Buddha!" Beyond wondering if you had stumbled into the wrong sanctuary, you'd want to convert the idolaters and show them the way of biblical truth. Yet when we are stubborn and demand our own way from the Father, He sees and hears us as if we were the ones kneeling and chanting in front of a cold and lifeless statue.

Love Waits for a Whisper

We need a word from the Lord. We need direction. We need to hear the voice of God. We need something that will stay with us next week and next month. The Word of the Lord is forever settled. "Heaven and earth shall pass away, but My words will not pass away" (Mt. 24:35). A Word from the Lord supersedes circumstances.

I will not tell you that walking with Jesus cannot be or will not be painful. Pain is inevitable. Misery, however, is optional. You are going to hurt. Life happens to all of us. Life is tough. Life is not always easy. If you want to be miserable about it, that's your choice. Both an optimist and a pessimist may make it to Heaven. The difference will be that the optimist enjoyed the journey. The thing that makes life bearable, enjoyable, and full of hope comes with the simple power of a whisper.

Jesus said, "If ye love Me, keep My commandments" (Jn. 14:15). Love precedes commandment keeping. If you try to keep His commandments without loving Him, you will find yourself in trouble. You will be miserable. If you love Him, your love enables you to keep His commandments.

Our Lord did not give Peter a lecture on how to feed sheep when He met him by the sea. Rather, He said, "Do you love Me? Do you love Me? Do you love Me?" Peter was nothing but a backslidden Christian on a fishing trip. But the Word of the Lord to Him was simple. "Love Me..."

The issue is the same today. Affection is the answer to apathy. Apathy is that I-don't-care spirit that invades us. If you love Him, you will feed His sheep. If you love Him, you will keep His commandments. If you love Him, you will love His Word. If you love Him, you will be waiting for a whisper.

There is going to be pain. Wind. Fire. Earthquake. You will wish God was in every bit of it when God is not in any of it. You are going to have to stay right there and watch it. But sooner or later the wind will die, the fire will go out, the earthquake will calm—and you will hear the still small voice of God. Oh, the power of a whisper!

A Whisper While the Storm Rages

When the disciples were in their boat caught in the storm, the Scripture tells us that Jesus "constrained" them (see Mk. 6:45). *Constrained* means He compelled them to get in the boat and go to the other side. They were seasoned mariners, sailors by trade. They probably looked at the sky and said, "There is a storm coming. It is not a good time to cross." But when Jesus says, "Go to the other side," it is time to go regardless of what the weather channel is predicting.

God told Joshua to cross the Jordan River even though it was harvest time and the waters were overflowing its banks. To the natural eye, it wasn't exactly the choice time to make the trip. However, when God says, "Go..." whether the circumstances look right or not, you'd better go. When you've got a word, go with it.

There are a lot of things in life that do not make sense. God gives commandments, but not always explanations, even when we want to know the why and the how and all the details. Sometimes He offers no further word.

If Jesus said "Go," they had to move. If He told them to "Go," they had to trust that He knew they would make it. Yet the storm came. The third watch of the night, which was about four o'clock in the morning, they found themselves in the midst of a storm-tossed Sea of Galilee. They were too far out to turn back, too far from shore to safely make it in before the storm. Can't you imagine how frantic they must have been—perhaps shouting orders to one another? "Man the sail!" "Somebody start bailing! We're taking on water!" Someone might have asked, "Should we abandon ship and hope to swim home?"

You'll hear all kinds of voices in a storm. You'll worry that you're off course. You'll question if you're going to lose the ship. But remember, that if Jesus said "Go over," He won't let you go under!

In the middle of their desperate efforts, they looked up and there came Jesus walking on the water. They were traveling with a word from the Lord, and now He was coming to their rescue. Anytime you sail into a storm doing the will of God, look up because Jesus is going to come walking your way. He will either calm the storm or calm you while it rages. Personally, I'd rather He calm the storm. But I've also been in situations when I knew He wanted me to "ride it out."

When they looked up and saw Him, they thought it was a ghost. Sometimes when you are in the storm it is difficult to recognize Him. But when you hear Him whisper, "Be not afraid. It is I" you will know it's Him. Apparently, though He spoke to all of them, not all of them heard. Peter said, "Is that You, Lord? Give me a word..." Someone with a hearing ear for a whisper above the clamor of life can expect a safe journey.

Jesus said, "Come..." There's a storm. "Come." The waves are high. "Come." The wind is whipping about. "Come." Peter stepped out and started walking toward Jesus. Have you ever thought that the thing that threatened to sweep over Peter's head (the sea) was already under Jesus' feet, so Peter could step out with confidence.

Whatever is threatening to be over your head—it is already under His feet. "Thou hast put all things in subjection under His feet" (Heb. 2:8a).

Peter started sinking. I can just imagine the conversation on the ship. "I told him it wasn't going to work" from doubting Thomas. Pragmatically John started, "I told him I'd already figured out that his size 12 shoes and 240 pounds of fisherman would definitely sink." But Peter hadn't listened to pragmaticism or skepticism or criticism. Jesus said, "Come," and he obeyed.

He had a word and proceeded accordingly. Anytime you are traveling with a word and start sinking, Jesus is there and is going to reach down and lift you up. Peter and Jesus then walked together the rest of the way to the ship. He will come to you! That is the power of one simple word whispered in your storm.

Sometimes you come out of one storm and it seems like you go right into another one. They came out of the storm that day and were met by two demon-possessed men. But the same One who took care of the storm dealt with the demoniacs. "If God be for us, who can be against us?" (Rom. 8:31b)

If you can just get a word from the Lord, all the demons of hell cannot stop you. Storms will not deter you. Circumstances will not baffle you. You have heard from God and with that whisper comes the power to pursue it.

The Whisper of Patience and Faith

Believers cannot be defeated. The devil does not have the power nor the authority to defeat the children of God. How can I say that when we see individuals who have failed? Look at those who have fallen into sin. Somewhere along the way, they quit. God did not fail them. If the enemy had the ability to defeat the saints of God, there would be no successes. No one would be saved. Jesus spoke prophetically and powerfully to Peter when He said, "...And the gates of hell shall not prevail against [My Church]..." (Mt. 16:18). You can throw in the towel. You can give up. You can walk away from Him. But the enemy is already defeated. If you want to, you can quit, but you are walking away from a fight that is already won. The enemy cannot defeat you unless you surrender and give up the fight. You have the power of the Word that stands against all the forces of hell.

Isaiah 62:6-7 reads: "I have set watchmen upon thy walls, O Jerusalem, which shall never hold their peace day nor night: ye that make mention of the Lord, keep not silence. And give Him no rest, till He establish, and till He make Jerusalem a praise in the earth."

The Word of the Lord said, "Don't give Him any rest until He establishes what He said He'd do." I didn't even know God rested. I don't know how He rests, but I know this says not to give Him any rest. If you have a word from the Lord, something He said He was going to do, then you have the ability to not allow Him to rest until it is accomplished.

A few years ago the Lord spoke to me with regard to this particular passage as it related to some specific things I was praying for and expecting from God. I studied it. I claimed it. I determined, "Okay, God—I will not give You any rest until You establish what You said You were going to do." I didn't understand it exactly, but I did understand the Word of the Lord in Isaiah 62 and I could say, "According to Your Word, as I read it in Isaiah 62, I am not giving You any rest until You establish these things You promised me."

Is there a situation in your life that you feel you've had a word from the Lord about but haven't seen the answer yet? Like the old song says, is there a mountain "you can't tunnel through?" Give Him no rest until He establishes a word in your life.

There was a time in our lives when my wife and I faced a real crisis in our ministry. I simply did not know what to do. We had access to a little cabin on a lake, so I decided to take a few days off and go there. I told my wife, "I don't know how long I'll be gone—maybe two or three days." During that time I prayed. I fasted. I felt sorry for myself and threw myself a pity party. I even tried all the disciplines I knew.

God only answers the prayer of faith. You can go on a hunger strike, picket the throne and call it a fast. But if you do not come to Him in faith believing, you haven't accomplished much at all.

Finally, one day sitting in the middle of the lake crying to God—not fishing—something happened. It was like the sky opened and a peace of Heaven fell out. (Yes, I spelled that correctly.) I heard the whisper of the Lord and received His word as peace and direction flooded my soul.

Now, don't misunderstand me. I didn't go home to find that our situation had suddenly changed. What happened there was that He gave me a word, and with it came peace. I received direction. I had a word that kept us and in the coming weeks things began to unfold. I understood it because I waited until I had a word, and then moved in that energy.

According to Ephesians 1:11b, "He worketh all things after the counsel of His own will." The word *worketh* means energize. He energizes all things according to the counsel of His will. When you get in the will of God, there comes an energy that you don't have access to beforehand. It is an energy and the power to endure, to complete the task at hand, to make it through whatever the situation you face.

Sometimes it is patience we need. Sometimes it is faith. These two words appear in the Scripture together ten times, and only in the New Testament:

> *Remembering without ceasing your work of faith, and labour of love, and patience of hope in our Lord Jesus Christ, in the sight of God and our Father...* (1 Thessalonians 1:3).

> *So that we ourselves glory in you in the churches of God for your patience and faith in all your persecutions and tribulations that ye endure...* (2 Thessalonians 1:4).

> *But thou, O man of God, flee these things; and follow after righteousness, godliness, faith, love, patience, meekness.* (1 Timothy 6:11).

> *But thou hast fully known my doctrine, manner of life, purpose, faith, longsuffering, charity, patience...* (2 Timothy 3:10).

> *That the aged men be sober, grave, temperate, sound in faith, in charity, in patience...* (Titus 2:2).

That ye be not slothful, but followers of them who through faith and patience inherit the promises... (Hebrews 6:12).

Knowing this, that the trying of your faith worketh patience..." (James 1:3).

Then in Revelation there are three separate references. Revelation 2:19 refers to the church at Thyatira:

I know thy works, and charity, and service, and faith, and thy patience, and thy works; and the last to be more than the first (Revelation 2:19).

He that leadeth into captivity shall go into captivity: he that killeth with the sword must be killed with the sword. Here is the patience and the faith of the saints (Revelation 13:10).

Here is the patience of the saints: here are they that keep the commandments of God, and the faith of Jesus (Revelation 14:12).

Faith is the force against the mountain. Patience is what keeps faith in the field working. When you lose your patience, your faith caves in. Put faith against the mountain—rush and hurry—and get anxious—and your faith will cave in. You'll start wondering whether you really heard from God or not.

Paul said, "Ye have need of patience, that, after ye have done the will of God, ye might receive the promise" (Heb. 10:36). You put

> FAITH IS THE FORCE against the mountain. Patience is what keeps faith in the working field.

your faith, which is the power of even a whispered word, against the mountain in your way. Then behind that faith put patience, and sooner or later the mountain is going to move!

In Luke 18:7-8 we read, "And shall not God avenge His own elect, which cry day and night unto Him, though He bear long with them? I tell you that He will avenge them speedily. Nevertheless when the Son of man cometh, shall He find faith on the earth?"

I have been there—crying day and night about some things. Have you ever been in the same boat? Have you found yourself harassing God about something? "Though He bear long with them, I tell you that He will avenge them speedily." It's been going on day and night. You've been crying. You've put up with it and put up with it and all of a sudden He says, "It's going to happen speedily." That doesn't make a bit of sense. He says "speedily"—but you've been bombarding Heaven until you're almost ready to drop from exhaustion. Why didn't He do it the first time we told Him about it? Why didn't He answer at our first cry? But no, in His wisdom and plan, He makes us bear with it—so He can show us what "speedily" means.

For four hundred years the children of Israel were in Egyptian bondage. They cried day and night. But in one night, three million were brought out of the land of Egypt. Speedily. They got out in one night.

God is going to send revival in the last days. He is sending a mighty and miraculous outpouring of His Spirit "upon all flesh." And it will come speedily. We have cried day and night for it. We have prayed patiently for it. And, speedily He is going to pour out endtime revival.

Whatever your situation is, put patience with your faith. I cannot tell you how. I cannot tell you when. I cannot predict why. But if you've got a Word from the Lord, in God's time He will bring it to pass.

The three Hebrew children were thrown in a fiery furnace because they would not bow to a heathen god. The king looks in and instead of three, there were four men in the fire. One day they are the off-scouring of the earth. The next day a decree is made: "There is no God in all the world like the God of Shadrach, Meshach, and Abednego." When God gets ready, He does it speedily.

You may have to bear with it. You may have to wait. You may have to believe in spite of outward circumstances and situations. The only influence the devil has over you is over your human will. If he can get you to quit, he wins. But if you say, "No" and hold on in faith and patience to the Word from the Lord you have received, you will be victorious.

There may be a storm that arises. The road you are journeying may not be an easy one. I can tell you that if you've got a Word from the Lord, and are patient, and keep your faith, it will come to pass just like He said it would.

Isaiah went in to the ailing Hezekiah and said, "Set your house in order. You are going to die" (see Is. 38). Hezekiah turned his face to the wall, weeping and wailing, "I am going to die and there's nothing I can do about it." Then God stopped the prophet before he ever got out of the king's courtyard and said, "Go back and tell him I'm going to give him 15 more years." So he went back to the king and delivered the message." The king said, "Prove it."

Now how can you prove that kind of thing? He said, "Make the sundial go back about fifteen degrees." Hezekiah was ready to believe instantly the bad report. But when the positive word came, he wanted proof. He was sure he was going to die; he wanted proof he'd be allowed to live. Human nature sometimes overtakes supernatural intervention. Something bad happens and the whisper you hear is, "I knew that was going to happen." But when something good is coming, we're afraid to say it. We don't want to confess it. Our faith is diminished. We are waiting for a wind to blow, the fire to fall, the earth to quake. Instead…He sends the power of a whisper— a whisper that will keep you when the wind dies down, and the fire burns out, and the earthquake is stilled. There is power in His whisper! What is He saying to you today?

Endnote

1. See 1 Kings 19:12 NIV.

Also by
T.F. and Thetus Tenney

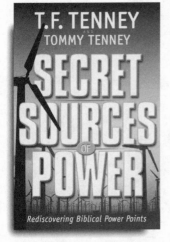

SECRET SOURCES OF POWER
by T.F. Tenney and Tommy Tenney

Everyone is searching for power. People are longing for some external force to empower their lives and transform their circumstances. *Secret Sources of Power* furnishes some of the keys that will unlock the door to divine power. You might be surprised at what is on the other side of that door. It will be the opposite of the world's concepts of power and how to obtain it. You will discover that before you lay hold of God's power you must let go of your own resources. You will be challenged to go down before you can be lifted up. Death always comes before resurrection. If you are dissatisfied with your life and long for the power of God to be manifested in you then now is the time. Take the keys and open the door to *Secret Sources of Power*!

ISBN: 0-7684-5000-4

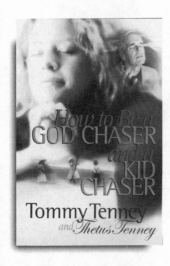

HOW TO BE A GODCHASER
AND A KID CHASER
by Thetus Tenney, et. al.

One of the great challenges for the modern parent is how to make room for your personal pursuit of God in the midst of the pressing priorities of raising a family. *How to Be a God Chaser and a Kid Chaser* offers many practical answers to this challenging issue. Those answers come from a diverse background of writers including Thetus Tenney, Tommy Tenney, Ceci Sheets, Cindy Jacobs, Beth Alves, Jane Hansen, Dick Eastman, and Wesley and Stacey Campbell.

ISBN: 0-7684-5006-3

Available at your local Christian bookstore.

For more information and sample chapters, visit www.destinyimage.com

Additional copies of this book and other
book titles from DESTINY IMAGE are
available at your local bookstore.

For a complete list of our titles,
visit us at www.destinyimage.com
Send a request for a catalog to:

Destiny Image® Publishers, Inc.

P.O. Box 310
Shippensburg, PA 17257-0310

*"Speaking to the Purposes of God for This
Generation and for the Generations to Come"*